MYTHS OF LOVE

Echoes of Ancient Mythology in the Modern Romantic Imagination

Dr. Ruth K. Westheimer

&

Jerome E. Singerman

Quill
Driver
Books

Fresno, California

Myths of Love
Copyright © 2014 by Ruth K. Westheimer
and Jerome E. Singerman.
All rights reserved.
Front cover image courtesy Alfredo Dagli Orti /
The Art Archive at Art Resource, NY

Published by Quill Driver Books
An imprint of Linden Publishing
2006 South Mary Street, Fresno, California 93721
(559) 233-6633 / (800) 345-4447
QuillDriverBooks.com

Quill Driver Books and Colophon are trademarks of
Linden Publishing, Inc.

ISBN 978-1-61035-211-6

135798642

Printed in the United States of America
on acid-free paper.

Library of Congress Cataloging-in-Publication Data on file.

MIX
Paper from
responsible sources
FSC® C011935
FSC
www.fsc.org

Contents

Introduction.................................v

Chapter 1: Tiresias
The Riddle of Pleasure and the Burden of Shame.........1

Chapter 2: Phaedra and Hippolytus
What Is This Thing Called Love?.....................5

Chapter 3: Cupid and Psyche
Love Discovered...................................12

Chapter 4: Leda and the Swan
Ceci n'est pas un cygne..............................16

Chapter 5: Helen and Paris
Lust and War.....................................21

Chapter 6: Laodamia and Protesilaus
Casualties of War..................................29

Chapter 7: Hermaphroditus and Salmacis
Love Denied......................................35

Chapter 8: Narcissus
Love Unshared....................................39

Chapter 9: Iphis and Ianthe
Gender-Bending Love..............................43

Chapter 10: Danaë
Pure Gold..50

Chapter 11: Pasiphaë and the Bull
Animal Lust......................................54

Chapter 12: Theseus and Ariadne
Seduced and Abandoned, Part I.....................56

Chapter 13: Dido and Aeneas
Seduced and Abandoned, Part II....................62

Chapter 14: Pygmalion and the Statue
The Art of Love or the Love of Art?....................70

Chapter 15: Canace and Macareus
All in the Family, Part I............................74

Chapter 16: Myrrha and Cinyras
All in the Family, Part II..........................79

Chapter 17: Venus and Adonis
Unexpected Changes................................85

Chapter 18: Pyramus and Thisbe
Missed Connections................................91

Chapter 19: Hero and Leander
Reckless Love....................................96

Chapter 20: Orpheus and Eurydice
Love and Loss...................................101

Chapter 21: Alcestis and Admetus
Lost Love......................................106

Chapter 22: Cephalus and Procris
Toxic Love.....................................113

Chapter 23: Acontius and Cydippe
A Marriage of True Minds.........................121

Chapter 24: Ceyx and Alcyone
Calming the Waters..............................127

Chapter 25: Baucis and Philemon
Love at the End.................................134

Reading Notes..........................138

Index.................................155

Acknowledgements.....................159

Introduction

"Only the lesson which is enjoyed can be learned well."
—*The Talmud*

This book is a collaboration between two good friends who first started talking to one another about classical mythology a few years ago, while in front of a painting by Lucas Cranach the Elder in the Metropolitan Museum of Art in New York. What we saw was this: In the foreground of an obviously Northern European landscape of conifers and rocky outcroppings, with a spired town visible in the distance and a fortress or monastery perched at the edge of a cliff, a young man is sitting beneath a tree. He is rather preposterously dressed in a full suit of armor accessorized with an elaborately tailored red velvet cloak. On his head he wears a gloriously wide-brimmed hat trimmed in feathers or fur. Standing in front of him are three women, naked but for the heavy gold jewelry around their necks and, atop the head of the figure in the middle, a hat to rival that of the young man. Interjecting himself between the young man and the ladies is a gray-bearded figure in extraordinary gold armor, wearing yet another piece of wonderful headgear— this a helmet seemingly made from two fully intact birds. Hovering in the air, in the upper left-hand corner, is Cupid, poised to shoot an arrow.

The painting is a famous one, but even had we been looking at it for the first time, the scene being represented would have been immediately recognizable. True, the period and the place are wrong and several key details are off. The man with the winged helmet is surely Hermes, but why is he so old? And why is he offering a clear glass orb when he is supposed to be holding a golden apple? Still, this is obviously a depiction of Paris judging the relative beauty of Hera, Aphrodite, and Athena in the prelude to the Trojan War.

One of us started wondering aloud about the tenacity and malleability of the Judgment of Paris story, and of classical myths more generally, as they changed and persisted over the millennia, about how these stories of gods and men from pagan Greece and Rome could remain such a part of the cultural landscapes of Reformation Germany and twenty-first-century New York alike. The other one of us zeroed in on the erotics of the scene before us, on the possible dynamic between Paris and the goddesses, and on how she herself was continually surprised by the ways in which the myths of classical antiquity so often help her to articulate her way of seeing the world.

And so we were launched. Wouldn't it make for an interesting project, we thought, to explore a group of myths from our individual and shared perspectives, perhaps even to write a book drawn from the conversations we anticipated having? We decided for obvious reasons to focus specifically on myths dealing somehow with the varieties of love—human and divine, licit and illicit, ennobling and debasing, gloriously fulfilled and tragically thwarted. Jerome Singerman could take the lead in selecting the stories and in bringing some knowledge of their literary, religious, and visual traditions to the table; but Ruth Westheimer would choose the way of retelling these stories and of coaxing from them their contemporary meanings. We are both very much the authors of this book, but it is Dr. Ruth's voice that you will hear whenever someone speaks here in the first-person singular.

It was, of course, no easy thing to make the selection of twenty-five stories you have before you, nor even to decide what was properly a myth and what not. We have been fairly generous in our criteria. These are stories overwhelmingly concerned with the loves of the gods or with the influence of the gods on the affairs of humans, although we admit that the connection is tenuous in one or two instances that are more exclusively tales of human love. And while some of the stories retain clear religious or cultic meanings, in others the gods are more appropriately taken as symbolic projections or perhaps even as narrative fancies. All of the stories we tell exist in ancient Greek or Roman sources, although some seem to be what we would consider individual authorial creations traceable to a single literary work. Others, of course, have deep and widespread roots in the ancient Mediterranean world, and in these cases, there tend to be significant variants between the versions. Even in antiquity, the overall shape and particular details of any given myth might be fluid, and we have often found ourselves offering bits of competing narratives within our retellings.

We have strived here to offer a selection that mixes the familiar and iconic—the usual suspects, you might say— with myths that may well be unfamiliar to many of our readers. There are inevitably omissions, and none seems more glaring, perhaps, than the story of Odysseus, the man who gave up the opportunity of eternal life to return to Penelope, the wife who remained faithful to him for the twenty years of his absence. It is, quite simply, a story we could imagine neither compressing into just a few pages nor extracting from the rich tapestry that is the *Odyssey*, a poem that is one of the greatest adventure stories of all times but also a veritable encyclopedia of many varieties of love beyond the conjugal. We have drawn from numerous other sources for what follows, though, and it will be clear that we have drunk longest and with the greatest satisfaction from Ovid. Surely it is no coincidence that he included so very many love stories in his *Metamorphoses*, for whether for good or ill, whether in antiquity or the present, there are few things in life quite so transformative as love.

A NOTE ON NAMES

Although the ancient Greek and Roman religions were not at all identical, from at least the third century BCE on the native Italian gods came to be identified with the deities of Greek Olympus. When the later Roman writers on whom we will draw—Ovid, Virgil, Seneca, the mythographer Hyginus—retold myths with roots in Greece, they routinely substituted their own gods for the originals. Thus Zeus becomes Jupiter or Jove, Hera becomes Juno, Artemis Diana, Aphrodite Venus, Hermes Mercury, Poseidon Neptune, Hades Pluto, and so forth. Of the major gods, only the name of Apollo remains the same in the two traditions.

In what follows, we tend to give the Greek form of the name when drawing primarily on a Greek original and the Roman form when using a Latin source. When important sources exist in both languages, we will often cite both names together.

1

Tiresias: The Riddle of Pleasure and the Burden of Shame

If you've ever seen or read the tragedy of *Oedipus*, you may remember Tiresias, the blind seer who tries to tell Oedipus that he has killed his own father and married his own mother. Now, in a book about myths of love, you may expect me to stop right here to talk about Oedipus himself, a mythological figure who had really serious love problems. Certainly, Freud thought this was one of the most interesting mythological love stories imaginable, and he based much of his theory of human psychology and sexuality on it. But Oedipus didn't know that the old man he had killed years before at a crossroads was actually his father, nor that the attractive older woman he later married was both the widow of the dead man and his own mother, so let's pass over him, at least for now. The fact is that it's Tiresias who really interests me, and I'd like to tell you why. It has to do with the way he lost his sight and gained his clairvoyance.

One version of the story has it that Tiresias was walking in the woods one day and saw Athena naked as she was taking a bath. The goddess, outraged at being caught undressed by a mortal, struck him blind to ensure that he never did this again. Zeus took pity on him, though, and gave him the gift of prophecy as a consolation prize.

The other version is far more interesting for us. One day, again walking in the woods, Tiresias came upon two giant snakes copulating. For whatever reason, he struck them apart with his staff and was instantly turned into a woman (in some accounts, it is Hera, the wife of Zeus, who does this, apparently angry that Tiresias has prevented the snakes from getting on with their business). Seven years later, the woman Tiresias is wandering through the forest again and sees the same two snakes, again in flagrante. Though you'd think she would have learned her lesson by now, she once again separates the snakes; perhaps she has learned *something*, because at least in some versions of the story she waits this time until they have finished. Whether that's the reason for what happens next, I won't venture a guess. In any event, Tiresias is suddenly transformed back into a man.

Hermaphroditus, whom we will meet a bit later on, was shamed by being both male and female at once. That's not the case for Tiresias (though he does show up in T. S. Eliot's *The Waste Land* as an "Old man with wrinkled female breasts"). What is so special about Tiresias is that he has been male and female in sequence. While this is now a possibility in these days of transgender surgery, it remained a subject of wonder until very recently. I don't know what readers would have found more fanciful when Virginia Woolf published her novel *Orlando* in 1928, for example. Would it have been the title character's remarkably long life, starting out as a Renaissance gentleman in chapter one and ending up in the twentieth century by the book's finish? Or would the greater surprise have been that somewhere in the middle of chapter three he had become a woman? I suspect the latter.

"Women have no desires . . . only affectations," a male character in *Orlando* says. Virginia Woolf knew better. Still, she could only imagine the differences between a man's and a woman's physical experiences of love and desire. People who have had gender reassignment surgery, on the other hand, can speak with personal authority to the physical and emotional change in their sexual response once the bodies they inhabit have been brought into closer alignment with their own sense of self. Still, however sophisticated the procedures for gender reassignment are, there are limitations to what surgery can accomplish. However godlike some surgeons think themselves to be, a sex-change operation performed by a real god (mythologically speaking) is something else entirely. So, I would argue, Tiresias may well be the only person on Earth ever to have been in the position of knowing who truly has the greater sexual pleasure, a man or a woman. And this is precisely what Zeus and Hera want to know when they try to settle an argument by asking Tiresias that very question.

Although the record is silent on Tiresias's sexual experiences as a man, he spent his years as a woman working as a prostitute with many partners, according to some traditions, and bore several children. (In Dante's *Inferno*, interestingly enough, Tiresias and his daughter, Manto, are cast into the same pit of hell, though Dante doesn't mention that the male Tiresias was actually Manto's mother rather than father). In any case, he responds to Zeus and Hera's question without any hesitation: Women derive far more pleasure from sex than men.

Outraged at hearing this, Hera metes out her favorite punishment and strikes him blind. Trying to balance the actions of his wife, Zeus once again gives Tiresias the gift of prophecy.

Were women in the ancient Greek and Roman world all so sexually fulfilled that Tiresias's answer is the obvious one? Somehow, I doubt it, but if I'm wrong, I'd say "Good for them!" Except that at bottom, this does not seem to be the response that the story is inviting. One would think that on hearing of women's greater sexual enjoyment, Hera would

> In one version of the myth, Tiresias gets rather specific in settling the bet between Zeus and Hera, declaring, "Of ten parts, man enjoys one only." How he came to quantify the difference between male and female sexual experience is anyone's guess.

have considered herself one of the lucky ones, would even have looked on her famously randy husband with a certain degree of pity. Instead, she is angry.

Does Hera's wrath only make sense as myth in a culture deeply ashamed of female sexuality? I am afraid so, and I am profoundly sad when I think that it is this same sense of shame that so many women throughout the world are still trying to overcome, so many thousands of years later.

2

Phaedra and Hippolytus:
What Is This Thing Called Love?

Wʜat is this thing, this love, of which they speak?"

"Sweetest and bitterest, both in one, at once."

This is Phaedra, the wife of Theseus, in conversation with her nurse in Euripides's play *Hippolytus*. That she is asking for a definition is a bit odd in one respect, because she is at this moment feeling herself very much in love's grip. But not so odd either, because what Phaedra is experiencing is a sexual longing so irrational, so passionate, and so overwhelming that she really has no idea of what has come over her. Unfortunately, it is not her husband whom she madly loves, but her stepson, Hippolytus. And the outcome will be tragic.

The myth is a simple one, at least on the surface. Hippolytus is the son of Theseus and the Amazon Hippolyta (or Antiope, in some accounts), now dead. Theseus has since married Phaedra, daughter of Minos and Pasiphaë of Crete (which makes, under the surface, for a rather complicated family dynamic, once you know that Theseus slew the Minotaur, the half man, half bull, half brother of Phaedra, and then seduced and abandoned Phaedra's full sister Ariadne; but more of that later). Phaedra's husband has been away for some time—four years, according to the Roman writer Seneca the Younger, in the play he based on this story.

During this absence Phaedra's behavior has been exemplary, until one day she is suddenly overtaken by a thing that causes her to lose strength, to stop eating, to become someone other than herself. Her old nurse wheedles out of Phaedra that the disease from which she suffers is a morbid lovesickness, and with great difficulty she even extracts the hidden identity of the beloved from her mistress.

Although the nurse has been sworn to secrecy, she either reveals Phaedra's love to Hippolytus directly or, in some versions, chats with the heretofore chaste, even prudish Hippolytus about the pleasures of sex, as a way of preparing him for the direct declaration of love from Phaedra that follows. Hippolytus responds with misogynistic outrage to these overtures and to the thought of Phaedra's proposed infidelity to Theseus. He loudly asserts his devotion to the virgin goddess Artemis (the Roman Diana) and flees the palace with a deep but misplaced sense of shame for having inspired Phaedra's lust.

In Euripides's version, an unhinged Phaedra now resolves to hang herself, but she takes preemptive measures to protect her posthumous reputation: She affixes a note to her body for Theseus to discover upon his return, falsely claiming that Hippolytus had raped her and that she has taken her life to preserve her honor. In later versions, Phaedra remains alive and makes these accusations in person to Theseus. Whether he learns of the supposed rape by hearing or reading about it, Theseus believes the story entirely, and how could he not? Phaedra has heretofore been a woman of irreproachable character and reputation. All too quickly and all too effectively, Theseus calls the curse of the sea god Poseidon down upon his son.

We learn what happens next from a messenger who now enters to report the horrific scene he has just witnessed. A monstrous bull has risen from the sea very near where Hippolytus was racing in his chariot and has caused the youth's horses to panic. Hippolytus loses control of the team, the chariot is overturned, and he is dragged on the ground by the frightened animals. His beautiful body is broken. Upon hearing this news, Phaedra (if she has not done so already) commits suicide, and Theseus recognizes that he has been deceived into sentencing his son to death.

Phaedra is one of the great dramatic roles for actresses "of a certain age" to perform, whether in Euripides's original or, maybe even more, in the great seventeenth-century French reworking of the material, Jean Racine's *Phèdre*. Indeed, if we are familiar with the story at all, we most likely assume Phaedra to be a woman well into her middle years, whose inappropriate desire is being directed toward a man much younger than she. But in fifth-century-BCE Athens, where Euripides's play was first written and produced, that would probably not have been the case. At whatever stage in their lives Athenian men wed, they tended to marry women of childbearing age, and second or third wives were often no older than their husband's children from a first marriage.

There is no problem then, at least early on in the tradition, of an unseemly age difference between Phaedra and Hippolytus; the two may well be contemporaries. But this had probably already changed by the time the story entered Roman literature in the first century CE, most prominently in Ovid's *Heroides*, a collection of imaginary love letters from mythological characters, and in Seneca's tragedy of *Phaedra*. She has grown older, while Hippolytus has remained the same age—hence, for example, her rather desperate need in Ovid to profess that her love is all the deeper and more passionate—and presumably, all the more exciting for her prospective lover—for having been awakened later in her life.

> "It is no longer a passion hidden in my heart: It is Venus herself fastened to her prey."
> —Phaedra, from Jean Racine, *Phèdre*, Act 1

In the more recent and rather brutal *Phaedra's Love*, by the troubled British playwright Sarah Kane, the age discrepancy is made explicit, when Phaedra is taunted by her daughter Strophe for being twenty years older than Hippolytus.

In spite of long overdue changes in our own attitudes, we still often raise an eyebrow when an older women goes out with a younger man, perhaps because we still dwell in the shadow of Freud—by which I mean that we inevitably seem to cast such relationships in Oedipal terms, even if only fleetingly. And certainly, especially once we have allowed the notion of an older and matronly Phaedra to take firm root in our minds, we are unlikely to be able think of the Phaedra and Hippolytus story without also thinking about it as a tale of thwarted incest.

Again, this was probably not the case in Athens, where, legally at least, there is no evidence that an affair between a stepparent and stepchild would have been seen in these terms. But things were different once more in Rome, and although Ovid's Phaedra may try to dismiss the transgression as trivial, every Roman would presumably have recognized that if Hippolytus had slept with his stepmother as she was trying to incite him to do, he would have been committing a criminal act of incest, punishable by banishment. In Racine, it is Phèdre herself who calls her passion incestuous. In Kane, the main characters themselves engage in a brutal and insinuating give-and-take, in which they never quite declare if what is going on is incest or not; the situation is less ambiguous to an anonymous bystander near the end of the play. "Raped his own mother," she says. "The bastard," her companion replies.

The great American playwright Eugene O'Neill was famously fascinated both by Freud and Greek myth in the 1920s and '30s, and while there are probably more differences than similarities between the play and the myth, *Desire Under the Elms* is often read as his version of the Phaedra and Hippolytus story, transplanted to a nineteenth-century New England farm. There is nothing vaguely maternal about Abbie, the play's sexually aggressive stepmother, though even at a comparatively young thirty-five, she is significantly senior to her stepson and lover Eben, the Hippolytus stand-in. Still, an atmosphere of incest lies thick over the action, as Eben fathers a child by his father's wife, a baby that is, then, at once both his son and his brother.

But in truth, as compelling a figure as Phaedra is, I think we miss out on the deep mystery of the myth if we focus too exclusively on her and on her predatory and possibly incestuous sexuality. Perhaps as she has been drawn to the center of the story, she has upset the dreadful balance it originally had. It is easy to forget that while in Seneca and Racine her suicide is the culmination of the tragic action and occurs very near to the end of the drama, in Euripides she actually dies at the midpoint, before the tragedy is fully played out. It may even be too easy to forget that it is not she but Hippolytus who is the title character in Euripides's play.

If the tragedy of Phaedra and Hippolytus is one of human sexuality gone wrong, it is not simply one of sexuality unbridled, but one, too, of sexuality denied. Racine, if I may say so, muddles this by providing his Hippolyte with a fiancée, Aricie. O'Neill diverges from the myth by making Eben not the falsely accused rapist but the real lover of his stepmother. And Kane's bleak rewriting of the myth is more radical still. Her Hippolytus is compulsively, joylessly, and vindictively sexual. When not pleasuring himself, he is summoning call girls to his room. Physically repellent (he is overweight and unwashed) and foulmouthed (a trait, in truth, he shares with the play's other unpleasant characters), he professes to "think about having sex with everyone" and engages in a graphic onstage sex act with Phaedra before cruelly sending her toward her death.

How different from the Hippolytus of the ancients, a figure who is resolutely, one might even say passionately, celibate. He would no sooner think of marrying or having recreational or companionate sex than of flying to the moon. His main activity and greatest pleasure is in joining the company of the virgin Goddess of the Hunt, Artemis. His point of pride is that he is the only male allowed to do so. I don't think that this is in any way meant to hint that he is effeminate, but it is not for nothing that he is the son of an Amazon mother. And when his father confronts him with Phaedra's written charges of rape, he responds in Euripides's *Hippolytus* with protestations of his purity:

There is one thing that I have never done, the thing
Of which you think that you convict me, father,
I am a virgin to this very day.
Save what I have heard or what I have seen in pictures,
I'm ignorant of the deed. Nor do I wish
To see such things, for I've a maiden soul.
—Euripides, *Hippolytus*, 2

The Greeks and the Romans idealized the virtues of self-control and moderation. It is a great and tragic paradox that in rejecting any form of sexuality (except, perhaps, for the most sublimated), Hippolytus may well have embraced self-control to an immoderate degree. One thing is certain: By devoting himself so obsessively to Artemis, he has scorned Aphrodite, the Goddess of Sexual Love. We will see over and again in this book that Aphrodite brings less sustained joy to humankind than one might hope or expect, but also that we are powerless before her. And so it is that in the prologue to Euripides's *Hippolytus*, Aphrodite herself makes an appearance and promises to lay waste to Artemis's protégé. Her means of doing so will be Phaedra, whom she has already caused to love Hippolytus for the sole purpose of setting into motion the chain of events that will lead to his death. Phaedra too shall die, but she is merely collateral damage; "Her suffering does not weigh in the scale so much," Aphrodite says.

What is this thing called love? It is sweet and bitter at once, as Phaedra's nurse says. And I'm afraid that often in Greek and Roman myth, it is the harsher flavor that predominates.

11

3

Cupid and Psyche: Love Discovered

It is funny how selectively we remember some stories, maybe filling in details that are not there in the original and forgetting many that are. Such, certainly, is the way my memory of the myth of Cupid and Psyche works, and I suspect that I am not alone. Perhaps you recall the story as I do: Psyche, a very beautiful and very young woman, finds herself in a mysteriously empty palace, where the servants are invisible, the table is set of its own accord, and music plays, though there are no musicians to be seen. Every night, under cover of darkness, the lord of the place comes to her bed unseen. The two become passionate lovers, knowing one another only—but fully—by touch, for he warns her she must never try to look upon him. If she does so, he will be lost to her forever. Every morning, before the daylight might reveal his appearance, he steals away.

> "Have you any wish ungratified? If you saw me, perhaps you would fear me, perhaps adore me, but all I ask of you is to love me. I would rather you would love me as an equal than adore me as a god."
> —Cupid, from Lucius Apuleius, "Cupid and Psyche," *The Golden Ass*

This goes on for some time, until at last curiosity, mixed with no small amount of fear, gets the better of Psyche. Why is her lover unwilling to be seen? What is his secret? What is wrong with him? Though he speaks gently and sweetly, perhaps he is monstrously deformed or, even worse, actually a monster. And so, one night, as soon as she is certain that he is asleep, Psyche defies her lover's prohibition by lighting a lamp. In its warm glow, he is revealed to her as Cupid himself, the winged God of Love. In love with Love, Psyche reaches out impetuously with one hand to touch him—and inadvertently tips the lamp she holds in the other. A drop of hot oil falls onto his naked skin, and he awakens with a start. She has broken the one prohibition he has placed on their love. He rises from their bed, beating his wings, and flies out the window. Psyche is left alone and heartsick.

The story of Cupid and Psyche is not really a myth in the way that most of the others in this book are, for it's actually traceable to one particular source, a second-century-CE Latin book called *The Transformations of Lucius*, though better known as *The Golden Ass*, and is probably the complete invention of its author, Apuleius. And when we go back to the original, we discover that the beginning of the story as I've just told it is not its real beginning, nor the ending anywhere near its real ending. So, what have I left out?

You have probably noticed on your own that the story already sounds more than a bit like the fairy tale of Beauty and the Beast (only sexier, and with a Beast that is one only in the heroine's mind). In fact, there's quite a bit more in Apuleius's version that anticipates what we've come to think of as the fairy tale. For one, the wicked sisters. Psyche has two, and though they're not *step*sisters, like Cinderella's, they might as well be. They are jealous of Psyche for her greater beauty and the greater wealth in which she lives; though both sisters are married to kings, they complain that they are *poor* kings, and old and tiresome, whereas Psyche's lover, though nobody has seen him, may very well be a Prince Charming. It is, in fact, the two sisters who plant in Psyche's mind the fear that the mystery lover may be a monster and who egg her on to break her promise by trying to look at him. And like the wicked stepsisters in Cinderella, they are punished for their iniquity; indeed, without feeling a bit of remorse, Psyche arranges things so that they plunge off a cliff to their deaths.

But the sisters are not the only ones who are jealous of Psyche, for in the original it is indeed jealousy that impels the whole story, and no one is more jealous of Psyche than Venus herself. It is Venus's jealousy that in fact first brings Cupid and Psyche together: The maiden is so extraordinarily beautiful and so well loved that no one is worshipping the goddess anymore. Like that of an aging film star, her fame is being eclipsed by the younger woman, and she is furious. She bids her son Cupid to shoot one of his arrows at Psyche and cause her to fall in love with someone disastrously unsuitable, but of course once Cupid sees Psyche, he has a different idea entirely and chooses her for himself. He does his best to keep the liaison a secret from his mother, but she finds out about it nonetheless (if you must know, according to Apuleius, a little bird tells her; perhaps this was less of a cliché in ancient Rome than it is today). Her jealousy goes into overdrive. Young Cupid has no right to leave his mother for another woman, she rails, much less to betray her with the very one she had sent him out to destroy. Venus rather melodramatically declares that Psyche has proved herself wholly unworthy of her boy, who now lies covered with burns, fighting desperately for his life. And when she finds out that Psyche, now wandering the earth in search of Cupid, is pregnant, she rages at the indignity of being exposed to the whole world as being old enough to be a grandmother.

But when I think of Cupid and Psyche, I forget all this anger and jealousy. I forget, too, that Venus makes sure that nobody, god or mortal, will give shelter to Psyche, or that when Psyche at last throws herself at Venus's mercy, the goddess viciously beats the girl, then sets her a series of elaborate and seemingly impossible, even deadly, tasks before Cupid and Psyche can be happily reunited at story's end (a reunion and happy ending I suspect many people also forget). No. What sticks in my mind is that this is perhaps the most sensuous and deeply erotic love story in all mythology. Two exquisitely beautiful young lovers come together in the dark and come to know one another not by sight but by touch. Their senses, their sexuality are awakened, hers for the first time, his as never before. But finally, what I take away from the story—and what I hope you will remember, too—is that eventually the sex alone is not and cannot be enough for Psyche. Great though it may be, she needs to know her lover better and differently: She must see him in the light, must know him for who he is, whatever the risks involved. Only when she does so can this passion mature into love.

4

Leda and the Swan:
Ceci n'est pas un cygne

Leda, wife of Tyndareus, king of Sparta, bore seven children I know of. Three of these, Timandra, Phoebe, and Philonoe, were presumably conceived in the most prosaic fashion, and though there is no necessary correlation, they are of little mythological importance. The twin boys, Castor and Pollux, are mentioned in both the *Iliad* and the *Odyssey*, sailed with Jason and the Argonauts to reclaim the Golden Fleece, and were transported into the heavens to become the constellation Gemini and the protectors of mariners after their death. Pretty good. The two other sisters, Helen and Clytemnestra, are notorious—Helen, for indirectly leading the known world into war, and Clytemnestra, for murdering her husband upon his return from that war. There is a certain confusion about the paternity of these four, and it is this, and the rather remarkable circumstances under which the children were conceived, that we most remember about Leda.

You see, though Castor, Pollux, Helen, and Clytemnestra were all siblings who shared the same mother, one cannot say with any confidence that they were born of the same womb. Let me explain this apparent paradox. Clytemnestra is most certainly Leda's daughter by Tyndareus, and Castor may or may not be Tyndareus's son as well. Pollux is almost always thought to be her child by Zeus—the twins, then, oddly enough, would actually be half brothers. And although the Greek anthologizer we know as the Pseudo-Apollodorus tells us that Leda had sexual relations with both Zeus and Tyndareus on the night Helen was conceived, there is general agreement in antiquity that it is the god rather than the mortal who is her father.

How then not of the same womb? Because Zeus came to Leda in the form of a swan, and it was as a swan that he ravished her. The biology may be shaky, but there is a perverse logic to the assumption that Leda would have given birth to their daughter not through mammalian means but by laying an egg. It is a rather ludicrous story really, and I suspect that at least some of the ancient Greeks knew that full well (in one variant, the egg is merely given to Helen for safekeeping by the goddess Nemesis). The earliest surviving reference to the hatching of Leda's child comes in the fifth century BCE, in Euripides's *Helen*, where the title character mentions the unlikely circumstances of her birth. On a fourth-century-BCE vase now in the archeological museum in Bari in southern Italy, Helen emerges comically from a cracked egg. Either she is an exceptionally well developed and handsomely proportioned infant, or the egg is gigantic, large enough to contain an adult.

By the early Middle Ages, the biology has become even shakier and the eggs have grown in number and fertility. According to the writer known rather grandly as the First Vatican Mythographer (though his only connection to the Vatican, apparently, is that a manuscript of his work is preserved in its library), Leda has laid not one egg but two, each containing a hatchling from two different fathers. Castor and Pollux are in one, Helen and Clytemnestra in the other. I have to believe that Leonardo da Vinci was having fun with the story when he created the painting that we know only from copies. A nude yet very domestic-looking Leda stands with her arms draped around a swan who stares up at her adoringly, while their family of four chubby babes plays happily in the eggshells from which they have just recently emerged.

The artists of the Italian Renaissance seem to have loved the story of Leda and the swan. Correggio places the couple at the middle of a jolly forest scene. Here, Leda is sitting in the shade of a tree by the edge of a pool or a stream, facing forward. The swan stands between her open legs, his neck curving upward between her naked breasts, his bill reaching just far enough to chuck her under the chin. She looks down rather sweetly at him. Were she only clothed she might be taken for the perfect affectionate pet owner. To the left, two infants play under the apparent supervision of an adolescent Cupid. To the right, a young girl is bathing in the water and she recoils from a swan that has swum up against her. Another female, this one a bit older and apparently more nubile, has just emerged from the water. A servant dries her with a towel, but she looks up—longingly? with pleasure?— at a swan that has just taken wing. It is a scene at once witty and gentle in its eroticism. Leda's is apparently not the only swan in the picture with sexual potential.

Michelangelo's version, like Leonardo's, is lost but often copied. There Leda was reclining in a pose that seems to have been borrowed from the figure of Night on his own Medici tombs. The owl standing beneath the crook of Night's sharply bended knee, though, is replaced by a swan nestled between Leda's legs. Its neck emerges northward and he stretches up to kiss, perhaps even enter her mouth with his bill. Tintoretto's version is more concretely situated and rather sly. Leda is semi-recumbent on a richly draped bed in her dusky chamber. She is naked save for the jewels around her neck and in her hair, and could easily be taken for the very image of a Venetian courtesan were it not for her avian companion. One arm is stretched out to cuddle the neck of the swan who stands on the floor by her side. Behind her, on the other side, a servant stands by a large cage that seems to have a permanent place in Leda's chamber. Is she trying to coax the bird back into his cage or has she just let the bird out to come to Leda's couch for what we must assume has become the mistress's anticipated and apparently habitual pleasure? It is unclear, but to its original viewers, this boudoir scene would have been unambiguously sexual.

I don't know of any Renaissance depiction that flirts with the pornographic possibilities of the story quite so openly as François Boucher's do in the eighteenth century. In one of his versions, the swan looks ever so eager to join in the twosome of a naked and rather surprised-looking Leda and the languorous unidentified female nude draped across her lap. But nothing matches the explicitness of his other painting of Leda. She is lying alone in bed on her back, her legs splayed, her sex exposed, and being obviously brought to pleasure by the swan who reaches in to penetrate her with his head and neck. Is there any painting from the Renaissance that actually depicts Leda being ravished or in anything like sexual ecstasy? I don't know of it, though I don't exclude the possibility that it may exist. Of one thing I'm more certain. None of the paintings I've seen give any hint of the dread consequences that will come of the coupling. For that, we either need to go back to Euripides's *Helen*, lamenting the violence that has been committed in her name, or await the arrival of William Butler Yeats's stunning poem "Leda and the Swan." In comparison to Yeats's apocalyptically charged eroticism, my Renaissance versions are positively serene.

But a few things are clear. For the artists of the Renaissance, Leda was a woman who loved her swan very, very much. And sometimes a swan is not simply a swan—by which I don't mean that sometimes a swan is just a god in disguise.

> "And how can body, laid in that white rush / But feel the strange heart beating where it lies?"
> —William Butler Yeats, "Leda and the Swan"

And that's quite obvious in some very curious medical illustrations of the following century that depict the elongated but obviously non-erect human penis oddly but gracefully curving—like the neck of a swan, perhaps? In one example I have in mind, the artist has even omitted any representation of the testicles, but has drawn a section of the legs flanking the organ so that they look very much like the outspread wings of the bird. I don't want to put too fine a point on it, but if all this is not quite as anatomically impossible as a woman who lays eggs, I nevertheless suspect that the two are very closely related.

5

Helen and Paris: Lust and War

There is probably no woman in all of classical mythology more famous than Helen of Troy, for it was over her, we are told, that the most devastating war the world had yet known was waged. To the degree that the ancient myths still hold meaning for us, the Trojan War will always be a symbol of devastation and upheaval without compare and Helen will always be the greatest beauty who has ever lived. I'm sure that there are many readers who would think it a serious failing if I were to omit from this book the story of Helen, her lover Paris, and what their passion unleashed. But is theirs truly a myth of love? I'm not at all sure.

You no doubt know at least the outlines of the story. Eris, the Goddess of Discord, was dropped from the guest list of a very special wedding party that was celebrating the marriage of Peleus, king of the Myrmidons, and the sea nymph Thetis. She appeared nonetheless, bearing a golden apple as a gift, not for the wedding couple but for one of the invited guests. The identity of the recipient was clearly inscribed on the apple, yet left purposefully ambiguous: "To the fairest," it read. She threw it into the assembly and left.

Now, this might set off a rather uncomfortable competition at any fancy party where a group of women were present, all hoping to be looking their best. You can imagine how much worse things can get if you're dealing with a group of vain goddesses. Each of the three—Hera, Athena, and Aphrodite—was quite sure that she alone was the intended recipient. Zeus, knowing better than to get involved here, deputized Hermes to find another judge. Hermes settled on Paris, prince of Troy, who was living as a shepherd on Mount Ida in Asia Minor (I'll go into the reasons for this in a bit). The goddesses went to him in a group, each in turn offering a bribe. If he chose Athena, she promised to give him wisdom and skill greater than any other mortal. If Hera was chosen, she would grant dominion over all of Europe and Asia as a token of her gratitude. But it was Aphrodite, the Goddess of Love, to whom Paris awarded the golden apple, not on the basis of her immense beauty alone, but because she also promised Helen as a reward.

There were, however, some obstacles to overcome. Paris and Helen lived in different kingdoms. Neither had ever laid eyes on the other. He was already married to someone else. She already had a husband. And each had already been marked for trouble.

In most versions of the story, of course, Helen was the daughter of Leda and Zeus. Still, Leda's mortal husband, Tyndareus, king of Sparta, assumed the role of father to her. When she was still quite young—a child in some accounts, or just barely of childbearing age in others—an adult Theseus, drawn by her divine paternity or her already extraordinary beauty, abducted Helen to be his bride. Sources differ on whether or not this relationship was consummated. Whatever the case, it shows an absolutely repugnant side of Theseus, though the ancients were apparently more unsettled by the political and dynastic implications of the abduction than by the taint of child abuse. This is hard to understand from our perspective, I know.

In any event, Helen was rescued and restored to her parents in short order, and grew to appropriate marriageable age (still quite young by our standards, of course). Kings, princes, and heroes came from all over Greece to ask for her hand. Theseus, apparently, was not among the suitors this time, but we know he would go on to serve other women ill. Still, Tyndareus feared a new round of trouble. Might one of the suitors, aware that Helen had already been abducted before, follow Theseus's lead and seize her for himself? Or might those angry and disappointed suitors who were not chosen turn violent and take up arms against Tyndareus once he had selected the bridegroom? Odysseus, the shrewdest of all Greek heroes, was present, and he proposed a solution to ease Tyndareus's concerns. All the suitors would take an oath swearing not to fight over Helen except in one instance alone: Should anyone be presumptuous enough to steal her away once more, all the kings and princes who had assembled would join together into a single allied force to vanquish the miscreant.

Menelaus was chosen as husband for Helen, and the others, true to their word, left peacefully. Tyndareus ceded not only his daughter but his throne, and Menelaus and Helen settled into married life as king and queen of Sparta. They were, themselves, parents of a daughter, Hermione.

And what of Paris in the meanwhile?

I am struck by how many of our favorite stories hinge on the prediction of a terrible fate awaiting a seemingly

23

innocent child and on the parents' doomed attempt to alter that future. A king tries to save his daughter from falling into a deathlike state of a hundred years' duration by banishing spindles from the realm, but she pricks her finger nonetheless and is lost to sleep for a century. Another king and his queen hope to foil the prophesy that their son will grow up to kill his father and marry his mother by committing infanticide, not counting on the fact that a stranger finding the exposed and mangled infant will respond only with pity and succor.

The story of Paris is closer to that of Oedipus than to Sleeping Beauty's. Shortly before he is born, Hecuba, his mother, dreams that she is giving birth to a flaming torch. Her child, it is predicted, will bring about not merely the death of his father, Priam, but the destruction of the entire kingdom. The only chance for Troy to be saved is for the baby to be killed. To whom do the king and queen bear the greater responsibility—to their family or to their people? They are faced with the most horrifying choice I can imagine. Priam and Hecuba hand the newborn over to their chief herdsman, Agelaus, with instructions that the infant is to be slain. The shepherd can bear to go only so far as to leave the child exposed on the slopes of Mount Ida to die, but Paris is saved by a she-bear who takes him to her lair and nurses him. Although Agelaus offers Priam proof of the infant's death, Paris actually survives, and Agelaus raises him as his own. Paris grows up to be a shepherd on Ida, but one of extraordinary beauty and intelligence. He attracts the attention of the nymph Oenone, whom he marries, and, as we have seen, of Hermes, Hera, Athena, and Aphrodite, as well. Shortly after he offers his judgment to the gods, he returns to Troy, where he is recognized by his parents, welcomed home and restored to princely status in spite of the fearful prophecy. And soon he equips a fleet of ships and sails to Sparta to claim the prize he has been promised.

Helen is taken off to Troy. Menelaus invokes the terms of the accord framed by Odysseus at the court of Tyndareus. And the entire Greek world gathers on the plains of Troy (also known as Ilium, hence the name of Homer's *Iliad*), where it lays siege to the city for ten years. In the

> "Was this the face that launch'd a thousand ships,/ And burnt the topless towers of Ilium?"
> —Christopher Marlowe, *The Tragical History of the Life and Death of Doctor Faustus*

end, of course, Troy is destroyed, but the victorious Greeks, too, suffer immense losses, both on the field of battle and afterward, as they attempt to return home. The world as it had been is overturned.

Now I know that Paris was not a real person, but I think I have a pretty good idea of what kind of fellow he is. He is clearly very good looking and undoubtedly quite charming and seductive (in most paintings of the Judgment of Paris, by the way, it is not only the goddesses who are half naked, but Paris too; Cranach is in a distinct minority in painting him as a knight in fashionable armor). He is also, in the end, lazy and cowardly, decidedly unheroic. Once the war that he has unleashed has begun, we are told, he spends most of his time indoors, allowing others, most notably his brother Hector, to fight for him. He is shallow and unfaithful, and has a wandering eye. He has, moreover, what we would call a real sense of entitlement, and acts without the slightest concern for the consequences. He knew about the prophecy

25

of the flaming torch, after all, just as he knew about the pact among the Greeks, and he took none of this into account. I'm afraid you have all met petty Parises in your lives. If you have been foolish enough to have had a romantic relationship with any of them, I suspect you came to regret it.

And what of Helen? Who was she? This turns out to be a far more difficult question to answer. In some versions of her story, Helen is swept immediately off her feet by Paris and goes off with him in the heat of passion. She is an equal partner in a hot, adulterous affair. In others, Paris has to work harder, wearing her down with cajolements and lavish gifts, before she willingly abandons her husband and daughter. She is inconstant and a bit of a gold digger, perhaps. In still other versions, she is raped by Paris and taken away by force. Here she is a victim of brutal sexual violence.

And what of her life in Troy? However it started, the affair or marriage with Paris generally seems to have soured. In the *Iliad*, she regrets the liaison and knows that future generations will blame her for the war. She is poignantly aware of her place in history. Nevertheless, her allegiances seem firmly with the Trojans, and she berates Paris for his reluctance to fight the enemy. In some versions of the story, when the Greeks enter the city hidden inside the Trojan Horse, she even tries to expose them. Suspicious of the gift, she circles the giant horse and attempts to trick them out into the open by imitating the voices of their wives. She has turned Trojan, in other words. But in other accounts, she rejoices at the Greeks' destruction of the city that has held her captive. On the last fatal night of its existence, she helps the invaders by sending them signals by torchlight and casts her lot once more with Menelaus, abetting him in the brutal slaughter of Deiphobus, the Trojan prince whom she married after Paris's death.

And of her life after Troy? In some versions she returns to Sparta with Menelaus and settles back into married life. In others, she is almost immediately taken up to Olympus to live with the gods. In one, she somehow ends up on the island of Rhodes, where she is killed by hanging, a violent end to a life that had unleashed massive violence.

There are so many different and competing stories of Helen that it is hard to know what to do with them. But this leads me to one last version. It is not the one most people tell, and it may seem surprising and even anticlimactic. But it is the one that makes the most sense to me, and the one in which I find the meaning I would like to share with you. Helen never went to Troy at all.

To be sure, Paris thought he carried her away, and he was certainly under the illusion that he lived with her as his wife. At the war's end, Menelaus believed that he had recaptured her and that it was she he was taking back to Sparta. But the Helen over whom they and the whole world fought was a mere phantasm, a hollow substitute made by Hera to undermine Aphrodite's victory. The false Helen has all of Helen's extraordinary physical beauty—and as no man ever looked to Helen for anything but her beauty, that is all that was necessary to carry off a totally convincing deception. The real Helen spent the years of the war hidden away in Egypt, much to her frustration, confusion, and sorrow. This is the person we meet in Euripides's play *Helen*. She is, actually, a rather full and sympathetic character who misses

27

her home and her family. She dreads the violence that her beauty unleashes in men, and spends much of the play in fear that the pattern is to be repeated, as the Egyptian prince Theoclymenus threatens to force her into marriage. She is horrified by all that has transpired in her name and knows what is at its root:

> *And so my life is monstrous, and . . . my beauty is to blame.*
> *I wish that like a picture I had been rubbed out*
> *and done again, made plain, without this loveliness.*
> —Euripides, *Helen*, 4

This Helen, who hardly shows up anywhere else in antiquity, is more than just her pretty face, and she realizes how different everything would be if only others would also recognize the fact. But Paris and all the others cannot look past her appearance. They mistake the face or the body for the person. And to my mind, they are not great lovers at all, but shallow fools of the sort that do an awful lot of damage in this world.

6

Laodamia and Protesilaus:
Casualties of War

I doubt that we know the name of the very first soldier to die in any of the wars in recent history, and sadly I doubt that we will have that knowledge for wars to come. But the ancients agree on the identity of the first Greek to die at Troy. He was Protesilaus, and we catch our earliest glimpse of him—and, more remotely, of the wife he left behind—in the so-called catalogue of ships in book 2 of Homer's *Iliad*.

Now, the action of the *Iliad* actually begins in the tenth and final year of the Trojan War, but here, early in the poem, we get a listing of all the Greek commanders who allied themselves with Menelaus to win back Helen, of where they came from, and of how many shiploads of soldiers they brought with them (I will leave it to others to count to see if the number really totals 1,000). The passage is a famous one that goes on for hundreds and hundreds of lines, and I bet I'm not the only one who finds it a bit tedious. Still, I recognize that it is an important part of Homer's epic poem.

About halfway in we hear about the soldiers from Phylacea, a region in Thessaly, who had sailed to Troy in forty ships:

Of these, fighting Protesilaus was leader while he lived; but now the black earth had closed him under, whose wife, cheeks torn for grief, was left behind in Phylacea and a

*marriage half completed; a Dardanian man had killed him
as he leapt from his ship, by far the first of all the Achaeans.*
—Homer, *Iliad*, 2

We have here a name and the bare bones of a story: an
eager and energetic commander now dead, a grieving and
self-lacerating widow, and a hint that they were newlyweds.
Additional details have come down to us from later writers.
I don't know if they are telling things that Homer's original
audience would have already had in the background or are
giving in to the temptation to embellish the outlines of a
received tale. I will leave that to the scholars to sort out. I do
know that I find this one of the saddest of myths.

Some of the fullest versions of myths that we have come
from the Roman poet Ovid. His *Metamorphoses* is a fabulous source, of course—almost an encyclopedia but much
more fun to read. Many people may be less familiar with his
Heroides, the series of poems composed in the form of love
letters from one mythological character to another. Mostly
it is the women who write—and the men who don't answer
(some things don't change very much). Often, the women
have been jilted by their lovers. That's not the case with
Laodamia, I'm sure, though we have only her side of the
correspondence.

She is writing shortly after Protesilaus has sailed off for
Troy, and even if she is a queen, she could almost be any
modern soldier's wife whose husband has been sent to
battle. She is clearly deeply and passionately in love with
him. She describes how she has no energy for doing her
hair or getting dressed up, how when friends suggest she try
to amuse herself, she takes no pleasure at the thought. She

vows to live austerely so long as her husband is at the front, in part because austerity seems appropriate in wartime, in part, it seems, because she has feelings of guilt:

> Should I arrange my hair while a great helmet
> weighs down his head? Should I put on new
> garments while he is burdened with heavy arms?
> Let them say I imitate your life
> Dressed coarsely; it is fitting for me to spend
> This time of war forsaking all joy.

—Ovid, *Heroides,* 13

She anticipates his return and describes in sensual terms the pleasure they will have once again in each other's arms. She tells him how she prays for his safe return—and how at any moment, she can experience sudden and terrifying panic: "When the war comes to mind it comes / with terror and my tears flow like snow that melts / in the sun."

If we can't be sure of how much Homer's first audience knew about Protesilaus's fate, we can be certain that Ovid's readers knew that things did not end well. Laodamia is writing to her husband at Aulis, where the Greek fleet is becalmed en route to Troy, and that in itself bodes ill. If you know your mythology, you know, of course, that the Greeks are stranded there because Artemis is angry at them, both because she favors Troy and because Agamemnon, the leader of the Greeks, has insulted her. The winds will pick up and the fleet will be able to sail again only after Agamemnon has sacrificed his daughter Iphigenia, a horrendous act that will eventually lead to his own death. But for now, Laodamia recalls that as Protesilaus was leaving to join his forces, he stumbled on the threshold. She may take it as a sign that he will return home, but even the most amateurish reader of omens can figure out that this means bad luck. Finally, Laodamia shares with her husband a bit of information in which we know both their fates are sealed:

I have heard of a prophecy that foretells
an unjust death for the Danaan
whose foot is the first to touch the soil of Troy.
Unhappy the woman who is first
to weep for a husband slain. May the gods keep
you from being too eager. Of all
the thousand ships may yours be the last to cleave
the weary surf. Also, let yourself
be the last to leave the ship.

—Ovid, *Heroides*, 13

By the time Ovid wrote Laodamia's letter, there was some confusion in the tradition about whether Protesilaus was the first Greek to die on the plains of Troy or the first victim on either side. In Homer, he seems to have been killed off directly upon leaving his ship; in other versions, he kills four Trojans before he himself is killed. Two things are agreed upon, however, by the later writers: that by being the first to set foot on Trojan soil, he had sealed his fate, and that he wasn't slain by any anonymous Trojan soldier but by Hector himself, the greatest (and most sympathetic) of Trojan heroes.

> "Unlucky is the first who will mourn her husband having been lost! May the gods make it so that you will not want to be too eager!"
> —Laodamia, from Ovid, *Heroides*, 13

Laodamia doesn't know this, of course, and there is something poignant in her writing to Protesilaus that she has heard of this Hector and that he is best avoided. But the Trojan army is full of Hectors, she goes on, and he should steer clear of them all. Hector now becomes a generic stand-in for all Trojan soldiers. Is that the only way we can think of the enemy and rationalize their deaths at the hands of our loved ones, by robbing them of their individuality? But the Trojan soldiers' new brides? Laodamia can't help but put herself in their place: They are so much luckier than she in that they still have their husbands nearby, but should anything happen to their men, the pain will be so much more immediate.

What breaks my heart about Laodamia in the *Heroides* is that although she doesn't realize it, we know that her whole letter is in fact a prediction of her husband's death. I don't know what is more painful: that we are powerless to turn him back or that we know the final outcome of the story, which is that she, too, will die. In one version, she simply throws herself on his funeral pyre. Another is far more romantic.

Protesilaus does, in fact, return to Laodamia. After his death, she is so distraught that the gods take pity on her. They release him from the Underworld for a span of three hours and the married lovers are reunited. I like to imagine that their meeting is much as Laodamia has imagined it in the *Heroides*: They make love tenderly and they talk, and they share all that they have experienced separately during his absence. Does Laodamia believe that he is permanently restored to life? That is unclear, but when the three hours are past and he returns to the world of the dead, her grief is even more intense than before.

There is one detail in the *Heroides* that is rather creepy. Laodamia writes to Protesilaus that she has had a wax effigy made of him that is so lifelike, that but for the fact that it doesn't speak, you would think it was Protesilaus himself: I gaze at it, I speak to it, I hold it to my bosom, she says. I think that particular wax dummy is Ovid's invention, and like so much else in his telling, it is surely there to remind us of what is to come, for in the other tellings she has the effigy made once she is widowed. Some say it is wax, some bronze, and her devotion to the effigy is so extreme as to cause those around her to worry for her sanity. She is no Pygmalion and her statue will never come to life. When her father spies her extreme devotion to it, he seizes the effigy and casts it into the flames. Laodamia leaps in after it to her death. Has she lost her reason and does she believe that it is Protesilaus himself whom she must try to save from the fire? Or is this simply the last and most desperate expression of a grief so great that she can no longer bear to live? I don't know. What I can say is that the myth of Laodamia and Protesilaus puts a very human face on the tragedy of the Trojan War.

7

Hermaphroditus and Salmacis: Love Denied

There is a Latin saying, *nomen est omen* (the name is a sign), and for no one in mythology is this truer than for poor Hermaphroditus, whose story is told by Ovid in the *Metamorphoses*. The child of Hermes and Aphrodite (that is, of Mercury and Venus), he had the beauty of both his divine parents and a name that was at once male and female, though he was not born with indeterminate or doubled gender. In the myth, Hermaphroditus was a young man of exceptional good looks but—surprising for the son of Venus—was untutored and uninterested in the ways of love. At the age of fifteen, he leaves the care of his foster mothers—the nymphs of Mount Ida—to see the world. After a time, he comes upon a beautiful, clear pool, the domain of the water nymph Salmacis.

Where her sister nymphs follow in the train of the hunting goddess Artemis (the Roman Diana), Salmacis cares for no such exertions. Rather, she prefers to stay by her fountain, bathing in its cool waters, admiring her own appearance in its reflective surface, resting on its green banks. Occasionally, she exerts herself so far as to gather flowers, and it is while doing this that she espies the beautiful Hermaphroditus and falls instantly in love. She approaches, asking him if he is Cupid himself, if he is promised to any other woman, offering herself as his bride. The uncomprehending youth rebuffs her advances. Undaunted, she begs for a kiss and tries to embrace him— but he threatens to depart the place immediately if she does not stop. Hermaphroditus seems to have no understanding of the erotic nature of Salmacis's attraction, nor of the effect his appearance has on her. Why else, having begged her once and for all to leave him alone, would he next strip off his clothes and dive naked into her waters for a swim?

The temptation is too great for Salmacis. Enflamed by her passion and losing all self-control, she too takes off her clothing and jumps into the water after him, wraps her arms around his naked swimming body, and furiously kisses and fondles him as he struggles to escape. The harder he tries to get free, the firmer her embrace becomes; he is like a tree being strangled by ivy, a marine creature crushed by an octopus's tentacles.

Still, Salmacis cannot make him yield. In desperation, she calls out to the gods, praying that they may never allow him to get away from her. Her prayers are answered immediately, and the bodies of Hermaphroditus and Salmacis melt together. No longer two, nor distinctly man or woman, they are at once neither and both. The world's first hermaphrodite is born.

"Amidst his limbs she kept her limbs entwin'd,
'And why, coy youth!' she cries. 'Why thus unkind?
Oh, may the gods thus keep us ever join'd!
Oh, may we never, never part again!'
So pray'd the nymph, nor did she pray in vain;
…Both bodies in a single body mix,
A single body with a double sex."
—Ovid, *Metamorphoses*, 4

We have come a long way from the story of
Hermaphroditus, and this is one of the myths of love on
which I choose to cast a very critical eye. For starters, we
now know that there is no such thing as a true hermaphrodite among human beings. Though there are some creatures
in the animal and insect kingdoms that are reproductively
both male and female, the people who were formerly called
hermaphrodites are now rather understood to be intersex,
born with genitalia and reproductive anatomy exhibiting
both male and female characteristics, neither fully formed.

In the past, overhasty if well-meaning attempts on the
part of parents or physicians to "fix" the situation by prema-
ture gender assignment or radical surgery have resulted in
tremendous unhappiness. There is much greater sensitivity
and understanding today, and a growing movement for
people born with sexually indeterminate characteristics to
embrace their condition, even as they may identify strongly
as either male or female.

They could not be more different from Hermaphroditus,
for though he has been transformed by an act of the gods,
the beautiful youth has had his double sexual identity
thrust unwillingly upon him. The fountain of Salmacis,
once known for its crystalline waters and softly verdant
banks, is turned by this story into a place of infamy. The
Hermaphroditus who inhabits it is an enfeebled and
grotesque being, and anyone foolish enough to bathe in the
pool after him will emerge equally weakened and emas-
culated. In the ancient myth, to be a hermaphrodite is
something shameful, to have gone from being fully a man
to being only half so. And here, too, is another reason that
I find this story so disturbing. It is not just that it projects

37

such a negative attitude toward the intersexed, but that it is deeply misogynistic as well: as Salmacis melts into Hermaphroditus, the greatest marker of his downfall seems to be not that he has become half a man, but that he is now half a woman.

8

Narcissus: Love Unshared

Why, I wonder, are some myths so much better known than others? I suspect that many of you are far more familiar with the story of Narcissus and Echo than with that of Hermaphroditus and Salmacis, yet I think of the two as companion pieces. Here once again a beautiful youth scorns the advances of a nymph and has a disastrous encounter with a body of water. We all know how the story ends: Narcissus, falling in love with the sight of his own reflection in a pool, pines away and dies, and his body is transformed into the nodding flower that bears his name.

I have to admit, something of a botanical rather than sexual nature has always puzzled me here. Narcissus is not a particularly likable fellow, yet there are few sights more welcome than the first daffodils (the common name for the narcissus flower) of spring. But no matter. The truths of the Narcissus story are to be found elsewhere, for in addition to giving his name to a flower, he gives his name to a behavior, and that's much more interesting to me.

The dictionary defines a narcissist as someone exhibiting excessive vanity or self-admiration, but that in fact is not how Narcissus starts out. For his problem, you see, is not at first that he loves himself but that, like Hermaphroditus, he loves no one. The nymph Echo is only one of many who long for him and is spurned—not, we may say, totally without reason, for Echo has a rather pathetically annoying trait we've all observed in needy lovers: Whether or not she has a thought of her own, all she does is parrot back whatever it is Narcissus says, as if nothing else mattered or existed. If he were a true narcissist at this stage, I suppose that might have been enough to win him over, but it isn't. He banishes her from his sight, and for this, at least, I really can't blame him. Would you be able to love someone so unable to hold up his or her half of the conversation?

Unlike the persistent Salmacis, at this point Echo gives up and more or less disappears from the story. In her sorrow, she wastes away, leaving as the sole remnant of her physical being the voice that repeats whatever words are spoken nearby. She seems not to be around when, as noted below, another would-be lover utters the prayer that will destroy Narcissus by being answered.

There was no stigma attached to certain kinds of homosexual relations in Roman society—more on that later—and it almost goes without saying that someone as beautiful as Narcissus would have attracted the passionate attention of male and female admirers alike. The Narcissus story has many problematic aspects, but its easy acceptance of this fact is not one of them. Narcissus spurns all his suitors with equal disdain. Among that sad rejected throng is an unnamed youth who plays a small but crucial role in the story. Crying out in pain to the gods, he asks no more than that Narcissus himself know what it is like to love Narcissus in vain. And the gods grant his wish.

One day, worn out after a hunt and exhausted from the heat, Narcissus kneels by a pool to drink. He is besotted by what he sees: a young man of extraordinary beauty, with flesh like marble and a face like a god's. As he leans in closer, the figure in the water approaches nearer. When he speaks, the youth in the water speaks as well. When he reaches out to touch him, the gesture is reciprocated. Their faces approach one another in anticipation of a first kiss—but the barrier of water keeps them apart.

As it is perhaps unfair to attribute an Oedipus complex to the mythic hero who didn't know he had married his own mother, so at this stage it is a bit unfair to ascribe narcissism to Narcissus: He doesn't, after all, realize that the beautiful young man with whom he has fallen deeply and passionately in love is his own reflection. But the love, even at this stage, is obsessive and destructive. Narcissus cannot take his eyes off his new beloved and loses all interest in anything else. He will not sleep and cannot eat, and he begins to waste away. The passion is destructive, and I wonder if, for the Greeks and the Romans, this is due at least in part to the fact that the lovers are so evenly matched. If the love between men is sanctioned—and, indeed, Narcissus doesn't even find it worth mentioning that he has fallen for a man rather than a woman—there are, nevertheless, strict boundaries we find hard to understand. The object of a man's affection was to be younger and less powerful than himself—a youth, even a young slave—and always the passive partner. The sexual relationship is a hierarchical one. That no hierarchy is established here—that Narcissus and his beloved are, in fact, the greatest of equals—might have seemed problematic to the ancients.

But of course, Narcissus does eventually understand that the young man in the water is his own reflection, and the thing that he loves is himself. You would think that might help, but it only makes matters worse. Another dictionary entry for narcissism is a clinical one, defining it as "the condition of gaining emotional or erotic gratification from self-contemplation," yet it is precisely at the moment he realizes that he is his own beloved that Narcissus's fate is sealed. When he repeatedly reaches into the water and fails to grasp the young man reflected there, he laments that he loves what he could not touch. Once he figures out that he is that young man, with a physical body well within reach, his sorrow and frustration only increase.

> "I am he. I sense it and I am not deceived by my own image. I am burning with love for myself. I move and bear the flames."
> —Narcissus, from Ovid, *Metamorphoses*, 3

Woody Allen once said that the nice thing about masturbation is that it's sex with someone you love. This is apparently not a thought that would ever occur to a character in Greek or Roman mythology—nor, presumably, openly acknowledged by real Greeks or Romans. Narcissus's self-love can never be consummated, and he dies chaste and in grief.

9

Iphis and Ianthe: Gender-Bending Love

As far as I know, the myth of Iphis and Ianthe appears only once, in the ninth book of Ovid's *Metamorphoses*, and it may well be Ovid's own invention. It is not a very well known story, to be sure, but it has a habit of showing up whenever scholars are looking for an account of the love between women in ancient Rome (though it is actually set in Greece). There are features of it that you might think of as very modern in the abstract: It's not only a tale of two women who fall in love with one another, but also one that starts with a case of gender misassignment and ends with a sex change (miraculous and mythic rather than surgical, but no matter). And I can tell you another story—apparently true and from the early twentieth century and also modern at first glance—that seems to reverse, but actually echoes, the Iphis and Ianthe myth in funny ways. But neither story is particularly open minded in the end, and neither is what I really think of as enlightened.

There lived on the island of Crete a poor but honorable man named Ligdus and his wife, Telethusa. When she becomes pregnant, Ligdus hopes for two things: that Telethusa would have an easy birth, as free from pain as possible, and that she give birth to a boy, for girls are troublesome and weak. Now, the first wish seems to reveal Ligdus as a sensitive and loving husband, a nice guy, but the second is abhorrent to us. And things only get worse from there: If the baby *is* a girl, Ligdus makes Telethusa promise she will put the newborn to death. Ovid doesn't actually seem to condemn Ligdus for this; rather, he presents him as acting in sorrow (he is weeping the whole time) and out of necessity. Infanticide was not unknown to the Greeks and the Romans, and although in the stories with which we are most familiar it is boy children like Oedipus and Paris who are left to die, in actuality, the victims were much more likely to be girls. Sadly, it has often been the case in poor peasant societies where people are barely able to make a living off the land that sons are much more highly valued than daughters for the work they are able to do.

In any event, Telethusa will have none of this. Distraught, she has a dream shortly before she is to give birth: There before her bed stands Isis, the Goddess of the Moon and of Motherhood (the appearance of an Egyptian god in a Roman account of a purportedly Greek myth is not as puzzling as it may seem; in the ancient Mediterranean world, the gods did not stay within fixed borders). Isis advises Telethusa to ignore her husband, instructing her to keep the child whatever its sex and letting her know that the goddess will be ready to answer her prayers in the hour of need.

The birth is a painful one and the baby turns out to be a girl. Ligdus does not get either of his wishes, then, but he doesn't know about at least one of the disappointments. Telethusa tells him that he has a son and he never discovers otherwise—by which we learn, I suppose, that in Ovidian myths at least, men never bathe their children or change their diapers. The child is raised male and is called Iphis, a name that can serve either sex.

My twentieth-century story is one that took place in Germany and was told in a book that became quite a cause célèbre when it first appeared in 1907 as *Memoirs of a Man's Maiden Years* (*Aus eines Mannes Mädchenjahren*), written by the pseudonymous "N. O. Body." Although a number of details were changed to hide the identity of the memoirist, the historian Hermann Simon has done a fabulous job of ferreting out the real identity of the author. He wasn't born a peasant but a good bourgeois, and he wasn't born female but what we would call intersexed—and what the ancients, as we know, would have called a hermaphrodite. In the archives of the town of Bad Arolsen (called Bergheim in the book), Simon has found that the record of the birth of a boy, Karl Baer, is an emendation, made some twenty-two years after the fact, of an original entry for the birth of a girl, Martha (Nora in the book). And it is as Martha that she was brought up.

In both cases, the ancient and the modern, things go along more or less smoothly until the child reaches puberty. People notice that Nora/Martha has an unusually deep voice and that she is rather too fond of science and roughhousing to be a typical girl, but she continues to make her way. Of Iphis we hear that she possessed a delicate androgyny and would have been considered lovely whether as a male or a female. The real problem comes when each falls in love with another girl. In Martha's case, the object of affection is a young Ukrainian woman named Hanna; in Iphis's, it is blonde Ianthe, an acquaintance since childhood and a perfect match in almost every way—or perhaps I should say in one way too many! The two are betrothed.

Ianthe's joy is complete as she looks forward to the marriage and its consummation. Iphis, still guarding her secret, loves just as passionately—and is horrified by her sexual longings for another girl. This is an abhorrent and unnatural thing, she tells herself in one of the monologues at which Ovid excels: A heifer doesn't love another heifer or a mare another mare; the ram mates with a sheep, the stag with a doe. In all the animal kingdom, she laments, there has never been a case of a female pairing off with another female (we know now this is untrue). Not even Pasiphaë's love of the bull was so monstrous as the love she feels for Ianthe; though it crossed species, it was at least heterosexual. Ovid may be having a bit of fun with this last example, but his disgust at what we would call lesbian longing is apparently not a joke, nor is it peculiar to him.

As we have seen, the Romans, like the Greeks before them, were more than tolerant of certain configurations of male homosexual behavior. Zeus was no less virile for his love of Ganymede, and the emperor Hadrian did not shy from commissioning untold numbers of statues of his beautiful male favorite, Antinous. The love between women was seen in an entirely different light, though. It is true that in archaic Greece, and on the island of Lesbos in particular, relations of a sexual nature were said to have been a regular component of female friendship. We find evidence of this in the gorgeous poetry of Sappho, who is said to have organized a cult of women on that island, dedicated to Aphrodite and the Muses—and of course the words "Sapphic" and "lesbian" have fully entered our language.

There are ample indications, however, that the Romans, or at least Roman men, had no toleration for this. They were mocking at best, disgusted at worst by the thought of one woman offering sexual fulfillment to another. The Italian historian Eva Cantarella reconstructs the Roman mind-set as follows: "By making love to other women, [lesbians] usurp a male prerogative: the right to dispense pleasure. . . . In the Roman imagination, female homosexuality could only mean an attempt by a woman to replace a man, and an attempt by another woman to derive from homosexual intercourse, quite unnaturally, the pleasure which only men were able to confer" (*Bisexuality in the Ancient World*, p. 170). Where a contemporary version of the story of Iphis and Ianthe might end with Iphis dropping her male disguise and the two young women embracing each other for what they are, this is an impossibility in the Roman context. Instead, something else impossible but far more acceptable occurs.

When the wedding of Iphis and Ianthe can be put off no longer, Telethusa recalls the promise of Isis to help and goes to the temple of the goddess to pray. The temple begins to quake and the statue of Isis on the altar seems to move of its own accord; from the moon-shaped horns that she wears on her head, beams of light emerge. Not knowing precisely what this portends, but taking it as more of a good omen than ill, Telethusa leaves the temple, joined by her daughter. As the two walk, the stride of Iphis grows longer, the complexion becomes ruddier, the facial features stronger. Ovid is reticent about describing other physical changes but sums them up succinctly: "You who but lately were a girl are now a boy! Go . . . rejoice with gladness unafraid!" Something miraculous has happened, and the wedding night passes in the most time-honored and conventional fashion. By the following dawn, Ovid tells us, the boy Iphis had won his Ianthe.

And what of our early-twentieth-century case? The more passionate Martha's feelings for Hanna become, the greater her distress. She is pitched into a deep and even suicidal depression at the hopelessness of their love: "We considered our future prospects. What was to become of us? There was no way out, and no salvation, so

> "But Iphis follow'd with a larger stride: The whiteness of her Skin forsook her Face; Her looks emboldn'd, with an awful Grace: Her Features and her Strength together grew, And her long Hair to curling Locks withdrew. Her sparkling Eyes with Manly Vigour shone; Big was her Voice, Audacious was her Tone. The latent Parts, at length reveal'd, began To shoot, and spread, and burnish into Man."
> —Ovid, "The Fable Of Iphis and Ianthe," *Metamorphoses,* 9

we decided to die." She goes so far as to procure morphine with which to kill herself from a young doctor of her acquaintance. When he makes a pass at her, she slaps him in revulsion. Is this the moment at which Martha recognizes her maleness? It is an almost comic scene but also a homophobic one. For N. O. Body, both male and female homosexuality are impossibilities.

The resolution to the story comes with the ministrations of another doctor—for in turn-of-the-century Germany, it is indeed the doctors who are gods. Martha has injured her foot jumping off a tram and the physician who comes to aid her finds her in tears. It is sorrow, not physical pain, that causes her to cry, she confides: "I told him the story of my childhood, the secret of my body, and spoke to him of the countless sorrows and humiliations of bygone days. ... 'If you wish to be close to your friend and you can secure a future for her, then go ahead and marry her,' [he responded]. 'You are as much a man as I am!' Only a minor operation, which he explained to me, was needed. . . . The authorities could not deny permission for my transformation, and then I could marry my lady friend with a clear conscience. It was as though dark veils had been torn from my eyes. The doctor was right. Physically, I was a man."

And so Iphis, the girl brought up as a boy, actually becomes a boy and gets the girl Ianthe in the end. Martha, brought up as a girl, turns out to have been a boy all along and gets his Hanna in the end. A very happy resolution on both sides, you will agree. But as a sex therapist, I am disturbed by the message lying not so far beneath the surface of each story, that the only happy ending possible is a heterosexual one.

10

Danaë: Pure Gold

The early Greek philosopher Xenophanes faulted humankind for imagining its gods to be too much like mortal men and women, wearing human clothing, having voices, faces, bodies like our own. In Thrace, the gods are thought to have red hair and blue eyes, just like the Thracians themselves, he observed; in Ethiopia, the gods are imagined with black skin. If horses and oxen had hands and could draw, then their gods would take the form of horses and oxen. The whole notion is absurd, he implies.

Of course, it is this very anthropomorphism that keeps the Olympians still so interesting to us today. We feel as if we can relate to the Greek and Roman gods and goddesses, with all their recognizable peccadilloes and power plays. It can seem a very bourgeois cosmogony, that of the Greeks and the Romans. Zeus/Jupiter often comes across as nothing so much as a middle-aged business executive, bored in his marriage and always on the philandering prowl. Except here's where Xenophanes gets one of the big details wrong. When he's being particularly randy, Zeus is more often than not imagined not as another man but as an animal. We're the ones who can also imagine the gods in bovine or other form. True, when he wanted to seduce the married Alcmene, he took on the appearance of her husband, Amphitryon. But he made love to Leda in the shape of a swan and he abducted Europa in the form of a white bull. And it seems to me these bestial guises make the dalliances of Zeus all the more vivid. This is animal passion that we are seeing unleashed, male sexual aggression uncontrolled by human reason.

Which is what makes one particular myth of how a shape-shifting Zeus ravished a mortal woman so very peculiar. I am thinking of the story of Danaë.

There was, in Argos, in a time ancient even by the standards of Greek mythology, a king named Acrisios and his wife, called Eurydice in some sources (though she is not the same Eurydice whom Orpheus followed into the Underworld) and Aganippe in others. They had one daughter, Danaë, but they were unable to conceive a male heir, and so they turned to the Oracle at Delphi for advice. She offered none of the hoped-for assistance, instead issuing a dire and unexpected warning: Acrisios would have no son of his own, but he would die at the hands of his grandson.

You and I have read enough myths by now to know that anyone who tries to prevent such a prophecy from coming to pass is doomed to failure. The mythological characters themselves, though, remain surprisingly clueless on this point. And so Acrisios attempted to foil the prophecy by making sure that his daughter would live and die a virgin. He locked her up in an enclosure—a tower room in some accounts, an underground chamber with a ceiling open to the sky in others. There she languished, until she somehow caught the eye of Zeus. The god entered her cell and impregnated her. Her father, still trying to avoid his fate, cast her and her newborn son out to sea in a chest. But fate, or the intervention of Zeus, spared the mother and child and brought them to the island of Seriphos. Its king eventually took Danaë for his wife, and her son grew up to be Perseus, slayer of Medusa and one of the greatest heroes of Greek myth. And Acrisios? One day he was among the spectators watching athletic games in which Perseus happened to be competing. The younger man threw a discus or a javelin (both versions are told), and it went horribly astray in the air, striking Acrisios in the head and killing him, just as the Oracle had foretold so many years before.

Now how was it, precisely, that Zeus ravished Danaë on the night Perseus was conceived? As you may know, he appeared not as a man or a beast or a bird, or anything at all we might recognize as a corporeal being, really. He came without any fixed shape or body and certainly without male genitalia. He was, on that night, about as far from the anthropomorphic gods at which Xenophanes scoffed as it is possible to be while still having any trace of a physical presence. He came to Danaë, that is, as a shower of gold, raining down from above.

It is, frankly, impossible to imagine what if anything Zeus might have derived from all this. In some way, he almost disappears from the scene and we are left with that rarest of phenomena in classical mythology: an image of sexual pleasure that focuses on the woman in a nonjudgmental way. In some of the earliest illustrations of the story that have survived, painted on Greek vases that date from the fifth century BCE, Danaë lies on a couch, partly undressed, with a smile on her face as a thin stream of drops of gold fall vertically down on her. She looks happy, if perhaps a bit passive. Later artists depict the scene with much greater sensuality. There are numerous paintings of Danaë from the Italian Renaissance showing her as a nude recumbent on a richly draped bed, in a pose often used in paintings of Venus. Titian painted her at least four times. She is posing languidly, her legs slightly raised and apart as the gold falls. In one, Cupid, his bow in hand and his work obviously done, looks back on the scene as he walks away. In the other three, Cupid is replaced by an old female servant who stands in the background desperately trying to catch some of the gold for herself as it drops, in either an outstretched apron or dish—presumably not for its monetary value.

Artemisia Gentileschi, one of the few woman artists of the period, painted the scene as well, and I don't know if I'm projecting or not when I say hers seems much more realistic than Titian's. But the most erotic version by far is that of Gustav Klimt, from 1907. We see one raised buttock, an erect nipple, a gorgeous, abstract pattern of gold entering between the thighs, and the face of Danaë, her hair luxuriantly spread on the pillow, her eyes closed, her red lips turned slightly up in pleasure. There is little ambiguity as to what this painting is about. I just love it.

11

Pasiphaë and the Bull: Animal Lust

Greek and Roman myths have more than their share of stories of animals engaging in sex with women. A bull rapes Europa and carries her off, a swan impregnates Leda. But in neither of these cases, of course—nor in others like them—is the animal what it seems. Both Europa's bull and Leda's swan are in actuality Zeus, as we know, taking on one or another of his many disguises to seduce mortal women while eluding the jealous gaze of his divine wife, Hera. Not admirable behavior on the part of the god, exactly, but by no means an indication that the ancients thought any better of bestiality than we do. It is one thing for a woman to have relations with a god in animal form and quite another to couple with a real animal. Which brings me to Pasiphaë.

Pasiphaë was the wife of Minos, king of Crete. Before he came to rule the island, Minos prayed to Poseidon, the God of the Sea, for a sign of his favor, and Poseidon granted him this in the form of a glorious, powerful, and pure white bull. Now, Poseidon expected something in return for the gift— namely that Minos would sacrifice the bull to him—but Minos could not bring himself to slay so fine an animal, and substituted another instead. Poseidon became enraged and decided to take his vengeance. Minos would be cuckolded, and in the most mortifying way possible: Pasiphaë would be made to betray her husband with the bull.

So the god caused Pasiphaë to burn with passion for the beast, and the unnaturalness of her lust is only underscored by the lengths to which she was forced to go to consummate the relationship. To attract the bull, she enlisted the services of the greatest of human artificers, Daedalus (this all occurred before Daedalus fashioned the wings with which he gave his doomed son Icarus a bird's ability to fly—another story, perhaps, that tells us that the line between human and animal is not to be crossed lightly). He constructed for Pasiphaë an apparatus in the form of a wooden cow, into which she inserted herself, and wearing which she tricked the rutting bull into mounting her and satisfying her desires.

From the commingling of Leda and the god-in-the-form-of-a-swan was born Helen, the most beautiful of all mortals. Of the coupling of Pasiphaë and the white steer was born the hideous and cruel Minotaur, a monstrous creature with the body of a man but the head of a bull, a creature so horrible—and, we can well imagine, so humiliating to Minos—that the king had him banished from sight. It was Minos who summoned Daedalus this time, and bade him to construct the most elaborate maze ever known to man, the Labyrinth, into which the Minotaur was thrust, never to emerge again, but not yet out of the picture.

Which brings me next to the story of Ariadne, the Minotaur's half sister.

12

Theseus and Ariadne:
Seduced and Abandoned, Part I

In my practice as a therapist, one of the most difficult issues is how to restore trust to a relationship when one partner has betrayed the other. On that matter, as concerns Minos and Pasiphaë, the mythological record is silent. But we do know that according to tradition they had a number of children together, one of which was a son, Androgeus.

There are a several different accounts in myth of how Androgeus died, but in all of them Aegeus, king of Athens, was complicit, and for this Minos exacted a bitter price: Once a year, or once every seven years, or once every nine (there are different versions of this as well), Aegeus was forced to send a cohort of the fairest young Athenians to Crete as a reparation payment. They would be thrown into the Labyrinth, where they would be torn to pieces and killed as soon as they crossed the Minotaur's path. The monster was now transformed from the symbol of Minos's shame into the instrument of his vengeance—and a sign of his cruelty.

After this had gone on for some years, Aegeus's own son Theseus volunteered to go to Crete to end the slaughter by vanquishing the Minotaur. To Aegeus, this seemed a certain death sentence for his beloved son, and so it would have been had Ariadne, another of the children of Minos and Pasiphaë, not caught sight of Theseus when he appeared before Minos and not fallen—shall I say?—madly in love at first sight.

> "No sooner did she lower from him her incandescent eyes than she conceived throughout her body a flame, and totally, to the center of her bones, she burned."
>
> —Catallus, "Poem 64"

This is the part of the story with which you are most likely to be familiar. Although it meant betraying her own father, Ariadne would contrive to help her beloved Theseus slay the monster. Before he entered the Labyrinth, Ariadne gave to Theseus the two things that would ensure his survival. The first was a sword with which to kill the Minotaur, the second a simple thread to help him to find his way out of the Labyrinth. All he needed to do was to unspool the string onto the ground so as to mark the path by which he penetrated the maze, and then follow the trail of this string to find his way out.

The plan worked perfectly, and Theseus emerged, safe and triumphant. The monster was no more and the cruelty of Minos was undone, and all because of the love of Theseus and Ariadne. The lovers fled Crete immediately, sailing off toward Athens.

A happy ending? Not quite, or at least not in any way you might expect.

It is almost always a mistake in Greek mythology for a princess to run off with a foreign lover, and always a bad thing to aid the outsider to defeat her own father, even when the outsider is as great a hero as Theseus seems and the father as unsympathetic as Minos. Just think of the story of Jason's capture of the Golden Fleece, one of the most glorious exploits in all mythology. To travel to the land of Colchis, where the fleece was being kept, Jason had built the *Argo*, the first ship in human history: Here then is the origin of all the sea trade and travel that defined the ancient Mediterranean world.

But having reached Colchis by ship, Jason could never have captured the Golden Fleece without the help of Medea, the princess of the land who, like Ariadne, sees the handsome stranger and falls immediately and passionately in love with him. Acting against the interests of her father, King Æetes, Medea (who also happens to be a sorceress) gives Jason the magical tools to overcome every obstacle between him and the prize. Like Theseus and Ariadne, Jason and Medea flee immediately following his victory and they marry.

But within a few years, Jason tires of her and leaves her for another woman. The sorceress Medea not only then murders her rival by sending her a poison cloak, but hacks her own two sons by Jason to bits and sets his palace on fire before she flies off in a chariot drawn by serpents.

The end of Theseus and Ariadne's affair isn't so bloody, but it's almost as dramatic—and it comes a lot quicker. Before they can reach Athens, the ship carrying Theseus and Ariadne sets anchor at the island of Naxos, and Ariadne goes ashore and takes a nap. When she awakens, Theseus and his crew are nowhere to be seen. She runs to the beach and from there, in the distance, she catches sight of the ship at full sail moving toward the horizon. Theseus has abandoned her on the otherwise uninhabited island.

Medea had helped Jason win the Golden Fleece by magic and utilized sorcery to wreak vengeance on her unfaithful husband. Ariadne had enabled Theseus to triumph in the Labyrinth with only the loan of a sword and the gift of a simple piece of string. Unlike Medea, she is no sorceress, and has no supernatural tools at her disposal with which to punish Theseus or make him return to her. All she can do is run up and down the shore frantically, tearing at her hair and clothing, unable to understand why the man she loves, and who she thought loved her, has treated her so barbarously.

In the wonderful old movie *Never on Sunday*, the optimistic heroine Ilya, charmingly played by the late Melina Mercouri, goes to see a performance of the ancient Greek tragedy *Medea*. As the drama ends, the camera pans the faces of the audience. Each is wracked with pain and sorrow, except hers. She is smiling. When she's asked why, she provides her sunny alternative ending to the story. She is convinced that Medea couldn't really have killed her children and her husband's fiancée. Jason must have come to his senses, returned to his wife and kids, and took the family off for a picnic by the seashore.

Ilya would have to work less hard to snatch a happy ending from the story of Ariadne. As she runs abandoned and apparently doomed along the shore, the god Bacchus (or Dionysus) appears, accompanied by his retinue of celebrants. Riding in to save the day in his chariot drawn by cheetahs, he is literally a deus ex machina, a god descending on a machine. He takes Ariadne for his own and marries her on the spot. She is turned into a celestial body, the crown she had been wearing now visible in the heavens as the constellation Corona Borealis.

I too am an inveterate optimist, and I wish I could feel better about this outcome. But I'm persuaded by the artists, poets, and commentators who have found real ambiguity in the end of Ariadne's story. Bacchus arrives with a huge crash and in the company of an unruly and grotesque group of followers. As usual, he is drunk and out of control. In the famous painting of the scene by Titian, his retinue includes a satyr entangled by snakes and a grotesque creature with the face and torso of a small child and the legs of a goat. Bacchus himself is strangely pale (is he about to be sick?) and seems to be startled by the fact that he is tumbling out of the chariot in which he has been standing, hurtling toward Ariadne in his nakedness (the pink silk wrap he has been wearing is now covering his privates and nothing else, and it looks about to fly off). But he is not half so startled as Ariadne. She turns to him, with an expression of what might well be terror, her right arm raised before her face in vain attempt to prevent the inevitable.

Is this a holy marriage about to take place or a rape? Is Ariadne, buffeted by her passions, any more in control of her reason than Bacchus? And was she any more in control when she first gave herself over to Theseus?

"But bright Bacchus hurries from elsewhere with his chorus of Satyrs and Silenes from Nysa, seeking you, Ariadne, burning with love for you.."
—Catallus, "Poem 64"

Has she lost her senses here on Naxos? Or had she already lost them when she ran off with a total stranger, convinced that she was in love with him?

Whatever is happening down by the shore this day, it is no picnic, I'm afraid.

13

Dido and Aeneas:
Seduced and Abandoned, Part II

You will notice that the heroes of Greek and Roman myth spend a lot of their time traveling around the Mediterranean world, and though they are men on a mission, they often leave time for erotic dalliance. Their love interests often fall into one of two categories. There are native princesses—Ariadne and Medea, for example—whom the hero seduces, carries off, and abandons, and there are the seductresses, who waylay the hero, perhaps even for years at a time, keeping him from pursuit of his duty. Odysseus seems to have been especially drawn to the latter type, for there are two such figures in the *Odyssey*—the nymph Calypso, with whom, though eager to return home to Ithaca, he lingered seven years until Hermes came to release him, and the sorceress Circe, who turned his men to pigs but spared Odysseus for her bed.

The Circe figure is especially compelling to later poets who transformed the ancient materials into their own. In the Italian Renaissance, Ludovico Ariosto rewrote her in his *Orlando Furioso* as the temptress Alcina, who temporarily ensnared the hero Ruggiero. Not long after, in his *Gerusalemme Liberata*, Torquato Tasso had the enchantress Armida hold the hero Rinaldo in erotic bondage, keeping him from his holy mission to free Jerusalem from the Infidel. At the end of the sixteenth century, the story crossed the English Channel into Edmund Spenser's *Faerie Queene*, where the sensualist Acrasia held Guyon, the knightly embodiment of Temperance, in thrall in her lush Bower of Bliss. If you are impressed that I can keep these sound-alike, look-alike characters apart, let me assure you that I can only do so by checking my notes, over and over. But it does give you a sense of how the myths persist, even as they travel and change.

It is pretty clear which side is supposed to win when love is pitted against valor, or sensuality against heroic action, in all these versions of what is basically the same story. Love saps the strength of the hero, even turns him oddly effeminate (always taken as a bad thing, without any questioning). The hero must always free himself to follow the better and nobler course. There is no ambiguity.

Except, perhaps, in the case of Dido and Aeneas.

As Virgil tells the story in his *Aeneid*, Aeneas is the son of the Trojan Anchises and the goddess Venus. He survives the destruction of his city and is commanded by his mother to go forth and found a new Troy, one that will be even greater than the old. He will do this in Italy, and it is of course Rome that she is talking about. War weary though he may be, Aeneas sets forth, and his task is not an easy one. He will face more battles when he reaches the new homeland (these are narrated in the second half of Virgil's poem, the so-called Iliadic *Aeneid*); and before he can even get there, he will travel for years, buffeted by the seas and the gods, and will have adventures that rival—or at least that are modeled on—those of Odysseus. And that is how he washes up on the shores of North Africa, where the city of Carthage is rising with Dido as its queen.

I am certainly not alone in thinking that Dido is one of the most formidable women in classical mythology. Like Aeneas, she is an immigrant, expelled from her homeland by forces beyond her control; even more than Aeneas, though, she has retaken charge of her circumstances. Upon the death of her father, the king of Tyre, she was to share rule equally with her brother Pygmalion (a different Pygmalion from the sculptor). He, however, has usurped the throne and murdered Dido's husband, Sichaeus (sometimes called Acerbas), in hopes of appropriating the latter's considerable wealth. Dido flees, managing to take a treasure in gold and a retinue of followers with her. Pygmalion gives up the chase when she makes a show of casting the gold into the sea in sacks. In reality, the bags are filled with sand, the gold safely stowed below deck. This is the first instance in which she shows herself to be more like the resourceful Odysseus than the rather stolid Aeneas ever will be.

The second example of her cleverness comes when she reaches the site of what will become Carthage. She petitions the native rulers, foremost among them the neighboring prince Iarbus, to grant her and her followers a parcel of land as large as can be encircled by the hide of a single ox. They readily agree, no doubt puzzled by what she might propose to do with so small a stake. But Dido cuts the hide into the thinnest of strips possible and sews them together end-to-end. The length is considerable, and the substantial borders of Carthage are thus established. (I realize that I am digressing from the love story, but can you see why

I'm taken by this character? She is tremendously smart, resourceful, and independent.)

By the time Aeneas is carried ashore at Carthage, Dido's city is a glorious construction site. The buildings that are going up are of masonry, and the roads are paved. A harbor is being dredged and a theater built. The city is being constructed politically as well as physically: Laws are being enacted and a senate is being chosen, all under the governance of an enlightened and beloved queen. This, the exhausted and storm-battered Aeneas thinks, is a place whose inhabitants are fortunate indeed; this is a city in which he himself would happily dwell. The sentiment is only magnified when he and his men are graciously welcomed by Dido.

Let me tell you what happens next, in purely human terms. It is a story that rings entirely true to me and one to which I imagine many of you can relate. As Dido and Aeneas spend time together, they find pleasure in each other's company. She is quite taken by his looks, his bearing, and the stories of his valor (it doesn't hurt that his reputation has preceded him; one of the first things Aeneas sees when he reaches Carthage is a bas-relief depicting the events of the Trojan War; he easily picks himself out in the sculpted crowd). For the first time since her husband died, Dido finds herself sexually attracted to a man and is both surprised and ashamed by the fact. One can assume that she was married off quite young and that the marriage was an arranged one (in some accounts her husband was also her uncle). Still, she thought she had given all the love she had to her husband and vowed to remain faithful to him until her own death. Now she is not sure.

She confides all this to her sister Anna, who offers what seems sound advice: Dido is still young and attractive and should not wear out her life in mourning. How can she close herself off from love or the possibility of ever having children? And pragmatically, Carthage is surrounded by potentially hostile peoples on the coast of North Africa, Iarbas especially, and is always vulnerable to attack from Phoenicia by Pygmalion. She could do far worse than to take as her consort a man to whom she is attracted, who is of noble, even semidivine lineage, and who is a renowned warrior to boot.

If Dido were a patient of mine, I'd be a bit worried about what happens next. Unused to being in any kind of relationship, she develops a fixation on Aeneas of a sort that is perhaps more appropriate to a teenager than to an adult. She hangs on his every word, she fawns over him; when he is not in her presence she can think of nothing else. She gets no work done, and as she is the queen and not a private citizen, there are serious consequences to her dereliction of duty; without her leadership, the dredging of the harbor stops, the city's walls and towers are halted in mid-construction, the military no longer trains.

Then one day Dido and Aeneas are alone. They are out hunting with the full courtly retinue, when there is a sudden thunderstorm. The two take refuge in a cave and there, as the thunder and lightning rage, they consummate their relationship. Dido, inexperienced as she is, takes this as confirmation of a permanent commitment. She now considers herself married to the Trojan and declares this publicly. The two begin to live openly as a couple. The situation is not displeasing to Aeneas and is greatly to his material benefit

(Dido is both wealthy and generous). Others, however, are less pleased and find the arrangement scandalous.

Things go on in this manner for some time until one night, when Aeneas remembers his mission to Italy to found a new Troy. He resolves on the spot to leave Carthage and, with it, its queen, but he apparently lacks the courage to tell Dido about his plans. He begins the elaborate preparations for departure in secret, but it is a secret hard to keep—he is, after all, readying whole shiploads of Trojan sailors. Dido confronts him. The scenes that follow are painful to recall, but ones to which most anybody who has been through the bad breakup of a lopsided relationship can relate. She accuses him of cowardice and faithlessness. He replies unconvincingly that he never meant to slip away without telling her.

> "O, no! The gods weigh not what lovers do.
> It is Aeneas calls Aeneas hence,
> And woeful Dido . . .
> Desires Aeneas to remain with her."
> —Christopher Marlowe, *Dido, Queen of Carthage*

Dido calls him two faced and doubts his divine lineage. She asks him if their marriage has meant nothing to him. Aeneas answers that they were never officially married and that this is her version of things, not his. She claims that with his departure, she is newly vulnerable to military attacks from without (he has no response). He will never deny his affection for Dido, he assures her, but if he had his choice, he would never have left Troy; barring that possibility, he must be off to his new enterprise in Italy. She curses him and wishes him a death by drowning en route. A short time later, she sends a message begging him to stay with her just a little while longer, so that she may get better used to the idea of his abandonment.

And then comes the part to which I cannot, do not want to relate. Driven to extremes by her grief, Dido has a great pyre built. She tells Anna that she is doing so on the advice of a sorceress who counsels that she burn the bed on which she lay with Aeneas as well as whatever possessions he has left behind, an act that will either bring him back or exorcise him from her life. Her purpose, though, is something different. She mounts the pyre and kills herself with Aeneas's own sword. Aeneas, already at sea, looks back to see the smoke from the burning pyre rising to the sky in a thick cloud.

That, then, is the story as I choose to remember it, but I've left out a very important level of detail. Aeneas has failed to reach Italy up to this point because Juno is the sworn enemy to the Trojans and is doing all that she can to keep him off course. Aeneas is so attractive to Dido because Venus is concerned that her son have a period of rest and relaxation and the best way she can think of to ensure that is to cause Dido to fall in love with him; she has sent Cupid to enflame the queen's passions, and even to drive her mad with love. The consummation of the relationship in the cave is Juno's doing; she knows that at some point in the future Carthage and Rome are fated to be lethal enemies and the only chance for preventing the destruction of Carthage, a city dear to her, is to prevent Aeneas from ever reaching Italy, so as to prevent Rome from ever coming into existence.

When Aeneas finally recalls his mission to Italy, he does so not on his own, but because Jupiter, growing impatient with the delays, sends Mercury down to spur him on. In Virgil's telling, the gods are very much present and acting at cross-purposes to one another. Dido and Aeneas are caught in the crosshairs, as it were. He turns into a cad so that he might become the founding father of an empire. She converts into a figure that is at once Calypso keeping Odysseus from traveling on to Ithaca and Ariadne abandoned on the shore of Naxos by an unfeeling Theseus. And it is all as it must be.

And yet Virgil is too great a poet to let Aeneas off the hook entirely, and Dido too extraordinary a character for us to be able to dismiss her too easily as a type. In the end, it is she who dismisses Aeneas and not the reverse. Dido kills herself at the close of book 4 of the *Aeneid*. Two books later, in another imitation of an episode from the *Odyssey*, Aeneas travels to the Underworld, to speak with the shade, or ghost, of his father and to witness a pageant of the glorious Roman future that lies ahead. But first, in the world below, he passes through the Field of Mourning, where he catches sight of Dido. He speaks to her movingly now, expressing his deep sadness for the pain he caused her, swearing he left her against his will and at the command of the gods. If he is asking for forgiveness, she does not grant it. Instead, turning away without a word, she retreats into the woods, where the shade of her husband, Sichaeus, awaits her, sharing in her sorrows and joined to her in love. In her silence, I think, Dido has the last word.

14

Pygmalion and the Statue:
The Art of Love or the Love of Art?

As the Roman writer Pliny the Elder tells it in book 35 of his *Natural History*, the art of sculpture originated out of an act of longing. There was, in ancient times, a potter named Butades who lived in Corinth. His daughter, whose name does not come down to us, was deeply in love with a young man who was about to embark on a long and perilous journey. Wishing to keep his image before her in his absence, she placed a lamp up to his face so that his shadow fell on the wall behind, and following the edges of this shadow she traced his silhouette. It is, in fact, in such shadow tracings that the Greeks and the Romans saw the origins of the art of drawing, but according to Pliny, Butades saw something more. Applying his clay directly to the wall, he modeled the face of his daughter's beloved in three dimensions. He then colored and fired this bas-relief, and so sculpture was invented.

It's a nice story, and one that speaks to a desire that art be both lifelike and long lasting. We don't know if the young man ever returned to Butades's daughter, but Pliny tells us that the sculpture survived at Corinth for centuries to come.

There are even more stories about the ability of painting, one of the sister arts, to trick the eye. The most famous is probably about the competition between the fifth-century-

BCE Athenian artists Zeuxis and Parrhasius to see who was the more talented. Zeuxis revealed his entry, a still life of grapes so realistic that birds came pecking at it trying to eat the fruit. Sure of his victory, he then asked Parrhasius to pull back the curtain that was covering his painting. Parrhasius replied that there was no curtain, but only a painting of one, which was his entry in contest. Parrhasius wins.

Now, wouldn't it be something if the painted grapes really did turn into fruit as sweet and juicy as they look, and if the painted curtain actually was so real that you could move its silky folds aside? Could it ever happen that a work of art might come to life? It could, in the myth of Pygmalion, though it is unclear which is the greater animating force, the sculptor's skill or the power of his love.

The fullest version of the story comes, again, from Ovid, though he seems to have taken many of its details from a lost work by a Greek writer named Philostephanus on the history of Cyprus, the island sacred to Aphrodite or Venus where the story takes place. In Philostephanus, Pygmalion is the king of the place. Ovid for his part says nothing about whether Pygmalion is king or commoner, but he does indicate that Pygmalion is a troubled and lonely young man. The Propoetides, a group of women who had denied the divinity of Aphrodite, have been punished by the goddess, who turned them into prostitutes, and although they have now been further transformed—turned to stone, this time—Pygmalion is so disgusted by their wantonness and consequently so ready to think the worst of all women that he lives alone and celibate. He finds his refuge in sculpting his own alternative to the filth and corruption around him in the form of an ideal woman made out of ivory. She is

71

more beautiful than any creature ever born, and so lifelike one would swear she was alive. For obvious reasons, the purity of the ivory woman is above reproach. And he falls in love with her. (In Philostephanus, as best as we can tell, Pygmalion is not the sculptor of the statue he holds so dear, and it is not the image of an anonymous if perfect woman, but of Aphrodite herself.)

Many later paintings and sculptures of the story show the statue standing appropriately enough on a pedestal with Pygmalion at its feet, but both Philostephanus and Ovid tell us otherwise. Pygmalion is constantly kissing the statue and pretending that she returns his affections. He embraces the statue and imagines that its flesh gives way under the pressure, even to the extent that he fears bruising her. When he is not dressing her up in women's clothes and jewelry, he is placing her naked in his richly draped bed.

> "I can't turn your soul on. Leave me those feelings; and you can take away the voice and the face. They are not you."
> —Henry Higgins, from George Bernard Shaw, *Pygmalion*, 5

Details such as these, especially if the statue is indeed an effigy of the goddess, are fodder for early Christian writers who rail against pagan idolatry. In fact, whatever details we know of Philostephanus's lost text come from two of the Church Fathers, Clement of Alexandria and Arnobius of Sicca, who perhaps take too much pleasure in describing how Pygmalion had turned the image of the goddess into little more than a sex doll.

Finally, one day it is time on Cyprus for the festival of Aphrodite. The whole island flocks to her temple to make offerings. When Pygmalion approaches the altar he stumblingly prays for the thing in the world he has come to desire most. What he asks for though is not precisely what he means. "Please," he implores, "may I have a wife just like my statue." "May I marry my statue" is what the goddess more correctly hears. The flames at her altar flare up three times, and his wish will be granted. Pygmalion returns home and leans over the ivory figure, still recumbent and insensate on the couch. He kisses it. This time it seems warm to the touch. He places his hand on one of the breasts, and it is not only in his imagination that the flesh yields. He feels a pulse beat beneath her skin. She opens her eyes and sees the sky and her lover for the first time. His work of art is no longer simply lifelike but fully alive. It is a glorious moment, no?

And yet, as we see over and again, the myths are never quite so simple, and I would like to leave you with a few second thoughts. If Zeuxis's grapes had been real rather than painted, they would have been eaten by the birds, or left to rot in their dish, and wouldn't have survived very long at all. As Pygmalion will no doubt learn, the perfect female form also doesn't remain perfect once it is converted from ivory into aging flesh and blood, wrinkles, warts, cellulite, and all. But maybe the animated statue isn't quite as alive for Pygmalion as we would like to hope. You will notice, she doesn't say a word and is never even given a name (I can hear someone protesting that everyone knows she is Galatea; but the name isn't attached to her until much, much later, probably some-time in the eighteenth century). And has Pygmalion really stopped thinking of her as his creation to continue to shape as he pleases? The ever-canny Ovid gives us reason to pause when he likens her newly softened form to wax that is easily molded and shaped by the thumb into any form one pleases.

15

Canace and Macareus:
All in the Family, Part I

If I had to identify the most clueless lovers in myth, Canace and Macareus would certainly be prime candidates, at least on the basis of the scanty information available. Our fullest version of their story comes from Ovid, as the eleventh epistle in the *Heroides*, and you could probably write a short book about the bits that are glossed over—as well as about what at least one of the lovers apparently does not understand.

Stripped of some of its more horrendous and melodramatic details, Canace's letter is almost something that a young girl today, finding herself in a similar situation, might write to her boyfriend. She is an unwed mother, you see, who has just this day given birth to a baby boy. She had been able to conceal her pregnancy from her parents. How this might be, I don't understand, but one reads stories in the newspaper from time to time about pregnant teenagers who manage the same. But now her father has found out and he has gone into a blustering rage that is all too typical of his character. He is, after all, Aeolus, the Keeper of the Winds, in some versions the son of the god Poseidon, in others a mortal king. Here he is endowed with no apparent supernatural powers, but with a murderous temper.

As Canace writes to Macareus, the father of her child, she recalls in naïve detail the story of their love. He is, clearly, her first and only serious boyfriend. She remembers how, when she first fell for him, she would toss and turn at night and lose her appetite from thinking of him. It is as if she is inventing the symptoms of adolescent lovesickness for herself, but her nurse, older and wiser, knew full well what was going on. You are in love, she declares, and Canace, blushing, stares at her feet and admits this is so.

One moment she is a virgin, the next she realizes she is pregnant. The nurse, a type we encounter frequently in these myths and surely an ancestor of the very similar character we know well from *Romeo and Juliet*, brings to Canace all kinds of abortifacients (she admits to Macareus here for the first time that she had tried to terminate the pregnancy), but the fetus is hardy and comes to full term. Canace is unprepared for the pain of childbirth and experiences a difficult labor, but the young father is there to coach her—not with anything so modern as breathing exercises, but by laying close to her and offering her encouragement. A healthy baby boy is born. All this Canace recaps for Macareus, as well as what occurred after he departed the birthing room.

The pregnancy was secret, the mother unwed and still living at home, the child illegitimate. There is still the matter to resolve of what to do with the baby. The nurse, of course, has a plan. She will smuggle him out of the palace by placing him in a basket hidden by fruit and olive branches, which she will pretend she is bringing to a temple as an offering. On her way out, however, and within earshot of Aeolus, the newborn begins to wail. The king snatches the baby from her and rushes into Canace's chamber, bellowing out about his daughter's shame and threatening her with physical violence. He holds the infant up for all to see and declares that the child will be made a sacrifice, not in a temple, but in the woods, where he will be exposed to be devoured by dogs, wolves, and birds of prey. We are used by now to the convention that whenever a child in a myth is left out to die, he is saved by a kindly shepherd. There is, however, no one who comes to the aid of Canace and Macareus's baby.

This brings us to the point in time at which Canace is actually writing her letter, and to the bloody end of the story. Aeolus has sent a servant into the chamber to deliver a sword to Canace. The message is clear: She has shamed herself and her family and now she must die by her own hand. She writes to Macareus to ask that he retrieve whatever can be found of their child's body so that it can be interred with her remains. She bids him to live on but never to forget her. She loves him still, and by the time he receives this letter, it will likely be stained with her blood.

> "If aught of what I write is yet blotted deep and escapes your eye, 'twill be because the little roll has been stained by its mistress' blood."
> —Canace, from Ovid, *Heroides*, 11

I've shared here almost everything I know about Canace and Macareus except for one rather important detail. They are sister and brother. Their love story is an incestuous one.

Now that you've recovered from the shock, an odd and obvious fact about Ovid's version may strike you. Aeolus is just as unaware as you likely were that Canace has slept with her brother and that the baby was born out of incest. The rage he feels and the terrible price he exacts of his daughter come without his ever knowing the identity of the child's father. I'm not quite sure what to make of this, for brother/sister incest was certainly taboo in ancient Rome, and Aeolus's violent actions turn our attention away from that issue.

It is true that brother/sister incest stood near the very center of Greco-Roman religion: Zeus (or Roman Jupiter) was both brother and husband to Hera (Juno), by whom he fathered Ares (Mars). He was brother, too, to Demeter (Ceres), with whom he sired Proserpina (Persephone). But Canace and Macereus are not Olympians, nor are they Egyptian pharaohs, who had married their close relatives, including siblings, in an attempt to keep their bloodlines pure. That practice had recently ended in Ovid's time with the final conquest of Egypt by Rome and the death of the ignominious Cleopatra, who had wed two of her brothers but had borne children by Julius Caesar and Mark Antony. Some few years in the future, the emperor Caligula would be said to have had incestuous relations with three of his sisters, and to have taken Drusilla, his favorite, openly as his wife; when she died, according to the historian Suetonius, he declared a period of public mourning during which it would be a capital offense to laugh, bathe, or dine in the company of one's parents, wife, or children. But Caligula was thought to be erratic, even mad, and his marriage to Drusilla placed in the same category as his proposal to make one of his horses a high-government official.

Much as I abhor the brutality of Aeolus, it is the openness and innocence with which Canace continues to express her love to Macareus that I find most unsettling. In what we know will be her final moments, she recalls his loving promise to her as she gives birth to their child: "You shall be / Your brother's bride; he who made you a mother / will also make you his cherished wife." And these words, she says, gave her life. Can we see elsewhere just the slightest hint of blame in her words to him? Can we intuit that here, as in most cases of brother/sister incest, the male was the sexual aggressor ("Brother, you loved me more than a brother should / Why was I more to you than sister?"). Perhaps, but I am not sure. If that is the case, it is not one Canace chooses to acknowledge.

Teenage mother, daughter of an abusive father, sexually ignorant, in an ongoing incestuous relationship, and accidentally pregnant—if there was ever a character in Greek or Roman mythology falling through more holes in the safety net at once, I can't think of it.

16

Myrrha and Cinyras:
All in the Family, Part II

Would Oedipus be quite so familiar a figure to us were it not for the writings of Sigmund Freud? In Freud's formulation of the Oedipus complex, all boys move through a stage in their psychosexual development in which they harbor fantasies of murdering their fathers and marrying their mothers. I'm not sure if I've met many men in my life who have admitted to such desires, and it's even unclear if the mythical Oedipus harbored these thoughts. That's a moot point, really. He did perform both deeds, whether he wanted to or not.

Freud also postulated a rather awkwardly named "feminine Oedipus attitude" by analogy, to explain how girls develop a deep resentment of their mothers and harbor the fantasy of becoming pregnant by their fathers. He later changed his mind about the usefulness of this formulation, but by then Carl Jung had long since named it the Electra complex, after the character in Greek mythology who incited her brother Orestes to kill their mother, Clytemnestra, in retribution for the murder of their father, Agamemnon.

The Electra complex has always been something of a poor stepsister to Oedipus and has never caught the modern imagination in quite the same way. I can't help but wonder if the problem has almost as much to do with the specific myth chosen to tag it as with Freud's later uncertainty about the complex's very existence. The Electra story is simply not a very good fit when you think about it. To be sure, Electra harbors matricidal thoughts, though in the end her brother does as well. And there is no room in her story for the fantasy or possibility of incest with the father, who is, after all, already dead. Really, the myth of Myrrha might have been a much better choice.

Myrrha was the daughter of Cinyras, king of Cyprus, and his queen, Cenchreis. When Myrrha had reached the age of marriage, the palace thronged with suitors seeking her hand, many of them appropriate in equal measure. To his credit, Cinyras refuses to make the decision for his daughter and asks Myrrha herself to choose a husband from the rich field of possibilities. The maiden looks into her father's face, is tongue tied, then bursts out weeping. The father comforts her, kisses away her tears, and asks her again what kind of a husband she would hope for. "A man like you," she responds—probably the most pleasing answer any father of a marriageable young woman can ever hear. She is still daddy's little girl, and it is perhaps too soon to force the marriage issue on his jittery daughter. He lets the matter drop for the time being.

But Cinyras has misinterpreted the conversation and the reason for Myrrha's distress. She has in fact just stated her preference quite concretely. It is her father and her father alone whom she loves, and in a sexual fashion.

Once again, the story is found most fully in Ovid, this time in the tenth book of the *Metamorphoses*, where the teller (it is actually Orpheus who narrates) leaves no doubt about the transgressive nature of this passion. Even Cupid emphatically disavows any role here; he says Myrrha must have been pierced not by one of his arrows but by a fire-brand thrust at her by one of the Furies, risen from hell for the purpose. Myrrha herself knows this love to be a crime, and yet, she asks, should not a daughter love her father? She knows it to be unnatural, and yet do we not see in nature that animals mate with their offspring? Do we not even encourage the practice among domesticated livestock to strengthen breeding lines? And are there not even some peoples among whom mother mates with son, father with daughter, all to strengthen the family bonds? Are the taboos against parent/child incest universal in human society or specific only to certain cultures? Might they even run counter to the laws of nature?

Myrrha does her best to convince herself that even in this particular, morality is culturally determined and that the differences between human and animal behavior are arbitrary and imposed. She doesn't succeed. In despair, she resolves to kill herself.

Help, of the most ambiguous sort, comes once again in the form of her devoted nurse, who happens upon Myrrha just as she is fashioning a noose around her neck. The old woman, who clearly cares deeply for her charge, is frantic and asks what could have happened to bring Myrrha to this point. The young woman doesn't answer. The nurse persists, looking for possible explanations. If Myrrha has gone mad, the nurse will heal her with charms and herbs; if someone has cast a spell on her, the nurse knows how to undo it; if the gods are angry, she will arrange for a temple sacrifice. She reminds Myrrha that she is fortunate in having a loving mother and father. Myrrha sighs deeply. The nurse natters on.

At length she intuits that her mistress is unhappy in love, and with someone her parents would find unsuitable. Myrrha says nothing. The nurse decides to help resolve the situation. Myrrha holds back still. When the nurse says that she can arrange things in such a way that even Myrrha's father will never find out about his daughter's secret lover, the girl grows hysterical. The nurse refuses to give up. She threatens to report the suicide attempt to the king and queen. She tries to wheedle the name of the boy out of Myrrha. Finally, the young woman cries out that her mother is blessed in her husband, and the nurse, in horror, understands everything. And faithful, misguided servant that she is, she carries through on her promise to help.

It is at this point that Myrrha is moved into position to supplant her mother in her father's bed. Ironically enough, the opportunity is provided by the festival of Ceres, the Goddess of the Harvest and of the Earth's Fecundity, the protectress of marriage, and the mother who had once descended to the Underworld in hopes of saving her daughter. For nine days, married women bring the first offerings of the season to the goddess; for nine nights, they are prohibited from having sex with their husbands. And so, on the first evening of the festival, Myrrha's nurse, turned from caregiver to bawd, approaches Cinyras, who is alone in his chamber and a bit in his cups. She tells him that a beautiful young maiden is desperately in love with him and eager to share his bed. How old is the girl, he asks? Roughly the same age as your Myrrha, she responds. Bring her to me, he commands.

I can't help but observe that the same middle-aged man who is likely to recoil at the thought of his daughter being involved with a man old enough to be her father, sagging flesh, hairy ears and all, is just as likely to think himself in the prime of life and attractive enough to appeal to a much, much younger woman. Has it always been so? In any event, at the darkest hour of

> "When she hesitated, the old woman took her by the hand, and, leading her to the high bed, delivered her up, saying: 'Take her Cinyras, she is yours,' uniting their accursed flesh."
> —Ovid, *Metamorphoses*, 10

the night, the nurse delivers a trembling and now hesitant Myrrha to Cinyras's chamber.

He is, perhaps, a gentle lover to her as he takes her virginity on that first night. When she leaves his bed, still under cover of darkness, she is already pregnant. She comes to him again on the next night, more easily it seems, then on the next night and the next again. Cinyras still has no idea of her identity. Finally, like Psyche eager to see the lover she has known only in the dark, Cinyras lights a lamp and holds it up to the young girl in his bed, now revealed as his daughter.

Horrified and in shock for what he has done, Cinyras grabs his sword and moves to slay the suddenly repellent Myrrha, once his beloved daughter, now loved in the wrong way. She avoids his blows and flees into the night. She runs and runs, and (though Cyprus is an island) somehow runs as far as Arabia. With each day, the child in her belly has grown heavier and her shame has grown greater. Defeated at last, she prays to whatever god will hear her, begging that her life may end but that she may be spared death. As she speaks, roots grow from her feet, her arms turn into branches, her blood turns to sap and her skin to bark. She is metamorphosed into a tree, but one ever weeping in sorrow and shame. Shortly afterward, the trunk of the tree splits open and the child of Myrrha and Cinyras's incest is born.

And do you want to hear something curious? There is redemption of a sort at this sad story's end. The sap that flows from the tree is myrrh, in antiquity one of the most precious of all commodities, burned as incense at funerals, constituted into perfumes, used to flavor the most highly prized wines. And the baby of Myrrha and Cinyras? You might have thought he would be monstrous, but he is Adonis, whose very name is synonymous with male beauty, a youth so preternaturally handsome that even Venus herself is undone for love of him.

17

Venus and Adonis: Unexpected Changes

The story of Venus and Adonis is at once one of the most straightforward of the myths of love and one of the most counterintuitive—and not just because it revolves around the fact that not even the Goddess of Love can love happily (though that's pretty remarkable when you think about it).

Once again, it is in Ovid's *Metamorphoses* that we find the version most familiar to us. The infant Adonis, born from the bark of the myrrh tree into which his incestuous mother had been transformed, is placed in the care of the wood nymphs who find him. He is a child of extraordinary beauty, and this beauty only increases as he grows into adolescence and early manhood. Eventually he catches the eye of Venus herself, and she is as enflamed by love as any mortal she has ever made to feel passion. This is no casual dalliance for Venus, who abandons all of her customary haunts and behaviors so that she might spend more time in her young lover's presence. She no longer visits the island of Cythera, where she first came ashore after being born of sea foam, nor the town of Paphos, sacred to her; she forsakes even Olympus and the company of the other gods.

She transforms herself, somewhat implausibly, into an outdoorswoman for Adonis, who is interested in hunting

> "Even as the sun with purple-colour'd face
> Had ta'en his last leave of the weeping morn,
> Rose-cheek'd Adonis hied him to the chase;
> Hunting he loved, but love he laugh'd to scorn."
> —William Shakespeare, "Venus and Adonis"

above all other things, and together the two pass the time of day in the chase for deer and rabbits. Indeed, with her skirts hitched up to her knees, and as mindless of the rocks and thorns through which she is ranging as of the beauty treatments she is skipping, Venus seems rather more like the virgin goddess Diana, the huntress, than herself. But Diana, of course, would have had no interest in bedding her hunting companion.

As a hunter, Venus knows her limits. She is frightened of the more dangerous game—wild boars, bears, wolves, and lions—that can easily kill, and she begs Adonis to be fearful of them as well. He is young and rash, however, and no more likely than any other adolescent would be to act safely when the opportunity for more risky behavior presents itself. And so, on a morning when Venus has at last torn herself away to fly back to Paphos in her swan-drawn chariot, Adonis goes out hunting with his hounds. He is following a trail that is well known to him when his dogs come upon a boar hiding in the woods. They root the creature out and Adonis gives chase. He throws his lance and pierces the boar's flank, but he fails to land a mortal blow. The boar charges at Adonis, who is no match at all for the animal's strength and speed. It reaches the youth, who is now terrified and running for his life, and plunges its tusks deep into Adonis's groin. The boar drops the lifeless and gruesomely desexed Adonis on a stretch of yellow sand. As the blood oozes from his maimed body, the sand is stained crimson.

From afar, Venus hears the cries of Adonis and turns her airborne chariot around. She rushes back to where he lies and grieves over the body as any mortal would. She tears her hair, rends her garments, and curses the Fates for allowing her lover to die. But Venus has certain resources that are not at the disposal of mortals. She declares that there shall be a memorial to Adonis and her grief, something at once fleeting and eternal: a red flower that will return every year but bloom only shortly before its petals are carried away by the wind. She sprinkles the spilled and drying blood of Adonis with nectar, and within an hour the first anemone appears. Which leads me to ask, is Adonis really dead? Or has the mortal Adonis been granted eternal, if seasonal and cyclical, life? And was he really mortal to being with?

The name "Adonis" is related etymologically to the Hebrew "Adonai," for "lord" or "master," and scholars agree that like the Hebrew term, it can take on godly significance. That offers a clue, of course, as does an alternative story about Adonis's childhood that we find in the mythological compendium attributed to the Pseudo-Apollodorus. Venus—or rather, Aphrodite, for we are moving backward from a Roman version to a Greek—first saw Adonis not as a youth but as an infant. She found him right after his birth and placed him in a chest for safekeeping, but unwilling or unable to care for him, she asked Persephone, the Goddess of the Underworld, to look after him temporarily. Persephone grew so attached to the child that she

87

did not want to relinquish him when the time came. (In this account, mind you, neither goddess seems to have had thoughts of taking Adonis for a lover; they are in the position of foster mother to child, or perhaps even mistress to servant or slave.) Zeus is brought in to adjudicate, and he declares as a compromise that Adonis shall spend four months of every year in the Underworld with Persephone, four months with Aphrodite up above, and four months on his own (although Adonis chooses to spend those four discretionary months with Aphrodite, as well).

In this configuration, the story of Adonis becomes one of cyclical death and rebirth, and it mirrors the myth of Persephone herself. For four months every winter she is forced to stay in the Underworld with Hades, and the world above is barren; she is allowed to live above for the remaining eight months, and the earth is fruitful.

At some level, then, it makes sense that Ovid's Adonis ends up as a flower. The figure, it turns out, had always been connected with fertility and vegetative myths, an association that can actually be traced further back and farther east to its origins in Asia. And there was, in fact, an annual festival held in ancient Athens called the Adonia that shows these associations were still very much alive in Greece. For several days every year, the Athenian women would mourn the death of Adonis and then celebrate his rebirth, all the while watering and tending their own Gardens of Adonis—apparently pots of fast-growing plants that would then be left to die at the festival's end.

But I don't want to lose sight completely of the Adonis with whom we started: the very human and very handsome lover of the very heterosexual Venus. That's also a part of the story, and indeed, that's what is most often represented visually on everything from Attic red vases to the luscious Renaissance and early modern paintings by the likes of Titian, Rubens, Veronese, and Poussin. So how is it that moving forward chronologically, today we so often code the figure of Adonis as gay? Think, for example, of where and how often the name is used for restaurants, hotels, or cinemas catering to a mostly homosexual clientele.

Certainly, his legendary beauty makes him an object of male as well as female desire, but there are other young men in antiquity known equally for their good looks. The mythographer Hyginus provides a partial listing of them under the rubric of "Especially Handsome Teenagers" in his ancient collection of stories and characters. In addition to Adonis, he names Endymion, Ganymede, Hyacinthus, Narcissus, Hermaphroditus, Hylas, and Chrysippus. Of these, three are famous for having been loved by other males—Ganymede by Jupiter, Hyacinthus by Apollo, and Hylas by Heracles—and although there is a hint in a surviving Greek fragment that both Heracles and Apollo considered themselves rivals for Adonis's affections, this doesn't seem to have been a very common story.

I wonder if it is not from Shakespeare that we get the association. His early poem "Venus and Adonis" is certainly one of his most sexually charged works, thanks largely to the increasingly desperate attempts, both physical and verbal, on the part of the goddess to seduce the young man. If Ovid remains tactfully silent about the details of their relationship, we don't at all doubt that they were intimate. Shakespeare, on the other hand, is quite explicit about the fact that they were not. Adonis has not the slightest interest in Venus and manages to repulse all her advances. He argues that at sixteen he is too young for this kind of activity. He claims that she has vulgarly confused lust with love. To entreaties that are among the most erotic in all of Renaissance literature, he responds that he would much rather be left in peace to go hunting. I suspect that I am not alone in thinking his priorities would be different were it Mars or Apollo attempting the seduction.

18

Pyramus and Thisbe: Missed Connections

The tale of Pyramus and Thisbe is really one of the more ridiculous love stories from classical mythology. You probably remember its outlines: The two young people live next door to each other. They are both (no surprise) extraordinarily good looking and have known one another since childhood. In time acquaintance turns to love, but their families are sworn enemies and the young people are forbidden from having any contact with one another.

Luckily, there happens to be a hole in the wall between the two houses, which also luckily nobody but Pyramus and Thisbe seems ever to have noticed. They take to having furtive conversations through the chink. As they can't kiss through the hole, they make do with kissing the wall itself. But eventually tiring of this poor substitute for real contact, they hatch a plan to flee the city and run off together. They will wait until night falls and each will slip out of their family's house. Now you might think that they would agree to meet on the street or around the corner, but then there would be no story. They decide to meet outside the city walls instead, at the tomb of King Ninus, by a pool of water, near a cave, beneath a white mulberry tree.

Thisbe is the first to arrive, and as luck would have it, she soon has company, but it is not that of Pyramus. A lioness, fresh from having killed and eaten some grazing cattle, her jaws still dripping the blood of her prey, approaches to quench her thirst in the pool. Thisbe panics—a reasonable enough response under the circumstances—and runs into the cave to hide. As she flees, she drops her scarf, leaving it behind on the ground. And now things start getting really implausible. If the lioness is drinking from the pool, you would think that the water would wash away the dead cow's blood from her mouth, but again, there'd be no story if that were the case. Instead, she finishes drinking, and as she slinks away, she sees Thisbe's garment. She grabs it with her teeth, mauls it and bloodies it, and then, evidently bored by it, drops it as she retreats back into the forest.

At this moment, Pyramus arrives, sees the lioness's tracks and the bloodied scarf, doesn't bother to look any further, and jumps to the conclusion that Thisbe is dead and eaten. He blames himself for her death, takes out his sword, and rather dramatically commits suicide. First he makes a speech, which Thisbe in the nearby cave inexplicably doesn't hear, then he stabs himself with his sword; his blood spouts out and stains the fruit of the mulberry a deep red.

And now Thisbe, oblivious to what has just happened, emerges from the cave. She's a bit confused and not sure that she's in the right place, because she is looking for a tree with white berries and sees one with red instead. But then she notices the dying Pyramus on the ground. I'm not at all sure that she figures out *why* he has killed himself (how could she?), but she professes her love and follows suit. Before she dies, she blames both her parents and his for the enmity that kept the lovers apart and hopes that she and Pyramus might be laid to rest in a single tomb. No one is present to hear, of course, but somehow the parents get the message and Pyramus and Thisbe share a single funerary urn beneath a mulberry tree that will forever be red.

I'm far from the first person to find the story silly, starting with the chink in the wall at the beginning and going right through to the cascade of coincidences and

"I will follow thee in death, for I have been the cause; and death which alone could part us shall not prevent my joining thee. And ye, unhappy parents of us both, deny us not our united request."

—Thisbe, from Thomas Bulfinch, *Bulfinch's Mythology*

misunderstandings that lead up to the end. At the simple level of the plot, it's just way too complicated to be plausible. Shakespeare has good fun with it in *A Midsummer Night's Dream*, where the only people not in on the joke are Bottom and the other rude mechanicals, rehearsing and then presenting their play of Pyramus and Thisbe as a tragedy—to famously comic effect. The musical comedy *The Fantasticks* plays with the story in a different comical way: Two fathers who desperately *want* their children to marry pretend to be sworn enemies so that the younger generation will rebel—and so end up doing precisely what the parents want.

But mostly, Pyramus and Thisbe—or at least their most famous descendants—have been taken more seriously. I'm thinking, for one thing, of Romeo and Juliet. Shakespeare didn't base his play explicitly on the Pyramus and Thisbe myth; rather, he took the details of his version, including the Italian setting and character names, from some slightly earlier English versions that are themselves versions of

Italian Renaissance accounts of the sad doings of the Montagues and Capulets of Verona. Thank goodness they all do away with the hungry lioness, though I'm not sure that it's all that much more believable for Juliet to take a sleeping potion that convinces *everyone*—not just her young lover, but her parents, her nurse, the whole city— that she is dead. The faked death of the heroine, followed by the suicide of the hero, followed by the real death of the heroine, all within a matter of minutes, is still pretty melodramatic, and it's no surprise that it ends up on the opera stage in the nineteenth century, first with Bellini's *I Capuleti e i Montecchi*, later with Gounod's *Roméo et Juliette*. For all its flaws, the story has certainly had staying power.

Now, whatever you think of Pyramus and Thisbe, or Romeo or Juliet, or Tony and Maria in *West Side Story* (also a version, of course), it is always the lovers who are at the center of attention and who are meant to have our sympathy. And it's true, in neither the Pyramus and Thisbe myth nor *Romeo and Juliet* do we ever learn why the families of the parents are at such odds. In *West Side Story* we do know the reason, and it is not at all a pretty one; it is ethnic prejudice pure and simple. In each version, it is the connection of the two lovers—rash but honest—that heals the wound and fosters reconciliation after their deaths. And that is all to the good (though one would certainly prefer "happily ever after" to "buried in the same tomb").

But I am a mother, and I sometimes put myself in the place of Pyramus's parents, or Juliet's. And it is when I do so, and only when I do so, that I find myself caring about this story, beginning to take it seriously, starting to see a different kind of complexity in it. My first thoughts then are how unimaginable the sorrow, and guilt, and horror of a parent must be if her actions have in any way led to the harm and, most unthinkably, the death of her child. My next thoughts are a lot more difficult to articulate.

I like to think that I am an open-minded person. At the same time, I care deeply about the cultural and religious values with which I was brought up, for which in my childhood my family perished, and which I have struggled hard to maintain in my lifetime to pass on to my own children. It has been a joy without measure to see these values once more flourish in the world around me.

Few things have been more important to me than the happiness of my children and grandchildren. But how would I react were that happiness to come into conflict with the values that I hold most dear? Tragic or absurd, the story of Pyramus and Thisbe is easy to tie up neatly at the end if and only if the differences between the two families are foolish or hateful ones. But what if the differences are meaningful, and if there is no right or wrong on either side? Do the parents of Pyramus and Thisbe have their own stories to tell? If so, the myth of Pyramus and Thisbe's love might become very complicated indeed.

19

Hero and Leander: Reckless Love

I have always been something of a risk taker, and I hope the day never comes that I stop taking chances. When I was much younger, I envied the turtle for his ability to withdraw into the perfect safety of his shell, until I realized that when a turtle is pulled into himself like that, he might just as well be a stone. In order to see the world around him and in order to move forward, he needs to stick his neck out. It's no doubt more dangerous, but the rewards can be immense. I can't begin to imagine how much I would have missed out on—in family and friends, in work, and in love—if I had sat quietly in a corner and always played things safe.

But there are some risks that are just plain stupid to take, and I'm afraid that the very romantic story of Hero and Leander offers an example. We know it most fully from a poem by an obscure Greek writer of the fifth or sixth century BCE by the name of Musaeus, though he was undoubtedly working from earlier sources. Ovid, too, compresses a slice of the story into a pair of letters in the *Heroides*.

At one of the narrowest points of the Hellespont, the body of water in modern Turkey that connects the Sea of Marmara to the Aegean and separates Europe from Asia, there stood the facing ancient towns of Sestos and Abydos.

There was, in Sestos, a temple sacred to Venus, where every summer was held a great festival in honor of the goddess and her doomed lover Adonis. The town would be thronged with celebrants, including many young people there ostensibly to worship, but really, it seems, to look over all the other young people, and especially those of the opposite sex. I imagine something similar to the scene on the promenade of any modern holiday resort, on any evening of the summer.

The most beautiful of the young women by far was Hero, a priestess of Venus. Many of the young men ogled her, commenting that she looked more like a goddess than a mortal as she processed through the temple precinct, or if a mortal, then more like the famed Helen than anyone else. But it was only with the handsome Leander, who had sailed across that day from Abydos, that she chose to make eye contact. Emboldened, he worked his way through the crowd, touched her stole, clasped her hand, and maneuvered her into a secluded spot in the shadow of the building.

The cult of Venus or Aphrodite was practiced in different ways at different times throughout the ancient world. As she was the Goddess of Love, I suppose it's not entirely shocking that in some places there were even temple prostitutes dedicated to her service. Hero is not one of these. In truth, I'm not at all sure what kind of priestess she could have been, or if the role she describes at all corresponds to any real historical practice. She explains to the handsome young stranger that she lives in an isolated tower located at the water's edge just outside the city walls, alone except for a dedicated old nurse companion. She is, as she also tells him, a virgin. Leander makes haste to point out the oddity of this and argues that her worship of Venus would be much more meaningful were she to engage with him in the activities that Venus most famously promotes. The sexual attraction between the two is obvious and intense, and Hero is quick to agree, though she points out the practical difficulties in making this happen. Her parents would never allow her to wed a stranger, and one from Abydos at that (by which we learn that whatever kind of priestess she is, marriage to the right person would be a possibility). Sestos, moreover, is a small place filled with gossips eager to pry into everybody else's business. If she and Leander are to become lovers, they must meet in secret.

Before Leander leaves that day, they formulate a plan. At night, Hero will light a lamp high in her tower. This will be visible to Leander over the Hellespont in Abydos and will serve as both a signal that he should visit her and a beacon to light his way. As soon as he can be certain that no one will note his absence, he will slip out of his parents' house and swim across the channel to spend the night with Hero, departing unobserved shortly before dawn the following day to return home the way he came. Only Hero's nurse can know of the affair. Why swimming is preferable to taking out a small boat is never explained. Perhaps a single swimmer late at night would be less noticeable than someone out in a skiff. Perhaps it simply seems the more virile way, or the more sensual (Leander will always swim in the nude). Perhaps if they had not rushed into things quite so precipitously, they would have devised a better plan. Instead, on that very night, Leander swims the Hellespont for the first time and he and Hero become lovers. He will return to her night after night as the summer wears on.

Now, it is not impossible to swim the Hellespont (or the Dardanelles as it is now known). In May of 1810,

> "It lies not in our power to love, or hate,
> For will in us is over-rul'd by fate."
> —Christopher Marlowe, "Hero and Leander"

a young Lord Byron swam the distance between the sites of Sestos and Abydos in slightly more than an hour in emulation of Leander, and wrote a poem about it. Exactly two hundred years later to the day, there was an organized Byron Swim for two hundred entrants to commemorate in turn Byron's commemoration of the mythic event. But as the modern swimmers learned, these can be cold and treacherous waters, and anyone wishing to cross the channel must fight against a strong north-to-south current that sweeps down from the Sea of Marmara toward the Aegean. Those of the Byron swimmers whose strength gave out before they made it fully across, or those who began to experience the symptoms of hypothermia in spite of the modern wet suits they were wearing on that spring day, were picked out of the water and brought to safety by escort boats. Leander, of course, had no such backup.

In Ovid's account, the tragedy that befalls the young lovers occurs when it is summer still, after a period of stormy weather has kept them apart for seven nights. In Musaeus, it is wintertime already. Hero has continued to light her beckoning lamp through the change of seasons, and Leander has plunged every night into the ever-icier waters, crossing to his mistress in spite of storm surges, snow, and frost. It would only have been prudent, of course, for Hero to look out to sea and note how rough the waters were, and out of concern for her lover's safety to extinguish the light in her tower until warmer weather and calmer seas had returned. But she is not prudent. It is beyond foolish for Leander to think of venturing forth naked and unaccompanied when not even a sailor will leave the safety of the harbor. But he is a fool for love, and a night with Hero is worth any risk.

In Ovid, Leander writes to Hero that if he perishes on his next attempt to swim the Hellespont, he hopes that she will find his corpse, weep over it, and acknowledge that he has died for love of her. Take that as a premonition, if you will, or as the words of an adolescent boy trying to impress his girl with his stupid romantic bravura. As it happens, he does drown on his next attempt, and when Hero sees his lifeless body washed ashore the next morning, she responds quickly not by caressing him but by leaping from her tower to her own death.

I often say that the most important sex organ of all is the brain. I'm afraid in that regard, and in spite of all their youth, good looks, and sensuality, Hero and Leander were very poor lovers indeed.

20

Orpheus and Eurydice: Love and Loss

Orpheus is a figure whose name is practically synonymous with the power of poetry and music. He was the son of Oeagrus of Thrace—either a mortal or a river god—and the muse Calliope, and he was brought up by his mother and her eight sister muses in what it would be an understatement to call a musical household. Apollo himself was a frequent visitor, and he gave the child a golden lyre and taught him how to play it. And so, you might say, a career in music was launched.

Let Orpheus sing to the accompaniment of his lyre in the ancient retellings, and the power of his songs will astound. All manner of creatures and things will be drawn in. Men and women, nymphs, birds, beasts, and fishes will surround him, lured by the performance. He will charm even the trees and rocks of the forest into dancing to his music. This sounds rather frivolous, but these are more than natural powers, and it is not surprising that Orpheus is emblematic of the connection that all humankind seems to feel between music and the sacred. More than just a poet, he is a religious figure, associated in antiquity with various cults of Apollo and Dionysus and especially with the so-called Orphic mysteries. The theology of these is complex and strange to us. If it is a small leap to understand the notion that an immortal soul is imprisoned in a series of mortal human bodies, the original myth at the heart of the mysteries seems very alien, even primitive. It tells how the god Dionysus/ Zagreus was dismembered and then eaten by the Titans before somehow coming back to life in a more recognizable form.

The Orphic mysteries seem distant indeed. What people are most likely to remember about Orpheus today is something much more human: that once, for the briefest of times, he was married to Eurydice. On the very day of the wedding, as we most often recall the story, she was walking through a field of tall grass with a retinue of wood nymphs in attendance, when she was bitten in the ankle by a venomous snake. In an alternative version, told by Virgil in his *Georgics*, she is not strolling but running to escape pursuit by Aristaeus, the rude God of Shepherds, Cheese Making, and Beekeeping, when she stumbles onto the snake. Her death came rapidly in either event, and she was ushered down into the Underworld.

Orpheus's grief was enormous. He could be seen at break of day alone at the shoreline with his lyre, mourning his dead wife in song. As day departed, he would be there still, singing. At last he roused himself, not to bring his period of mourning to an end by returning home and resuming his life, but by trying to enact one of the most perennial and heart-piercing of human fantasies. He would go down to the Underworld to reclaim Eurydice. She could not possibly remain dead. He would bring her back to life.

In Greek and Roman mythology, the Underworld has a physical presence, with at least one fixed point of entry from the world above. If access is difficult for the living, egress is all but impossible. You can probably count on your fingers the number of figures in mythology who manage this escape, but Orpheus forges on. Just as he was able to charm the wild animals in the world above with his song, so is he able to lull Cerberus, the three-headed guard dog of Hades, to his will. He plays and sings for the dread Charon, who ferries him across the Acheron, the river of death. And he penetrates deeper into Hades, passing untold numbers of shades of the dead. Some walk quietly in groups, others experience horrible and eternal torment. There are bands of unwed maidens, and youths whose bodies have been consigned to funeral pyres. There are Sisyphus, forever rolling his boulder upward in punishment, and Ixion, bound for all time to an ever-spinning wheel of pain. All stop transfixed at the music of Orpheus.

He at last reaches his destination, the court of Hades and Persephone, king and queen of the Underworld, and pleads his case in song. He does not ask that Eurydice be permanently loosed from the bonds of death; he knows that both he and she must ultimately return to this place for good. But Eurydice has come here before her allotted time. May she be allowed to enjoy more of her life on earth. The inhabitants of the halls of death are awestruck, and Hades and Persephone are won over by his music and his eloquence. They grant his request, with one rather arbitrary seeming condition. Orpheus shall lead the way out of the Underworld, but Eurydice must follow in silence, several steps behind. Should he turn to look back at her before they emerge, she will be separated from him once more.

And this, of course, is what happens. When they are very near to the surface of the world that we know, Orpheus is seized with fear that Eurydice may no longer be walking behind him. Or perhaps it is that he can hold off no longer from looking on the face of the woman he loves, now so miraculously restored to him. For one reason or another, he turns around and a thunderous crash seems to shake the whole of the Underworld. Eurydice cries out that she is lost and he reaches out to grab her, but to no avail. She is gone, disappearing like smoke into the air.

> "At once she slipped away—
> and down. His arms stretched out convulsively
> to clasp and to be clasped in turn, but there
> was nothing but the unresisting air."
> —Ovid, *Metamorphoses*, 10

We like to put neat endings on the most familiar myths, and this is the point at which we usually conclude our telling or remembering of the Orpheus story. There is a sequel however, and one that is probably as horrifying to us in the modern world as it was essential to the myth's cultic meaning in antiquity. So let us continue to the real end.

Having lost Eurydice a second time, Orpheus's grief is even greater than before. He begs reentry to the Underworld to renew his quest and is denied access. For days after, he does not move. He neither eats nor drinks nor washes. When he stirs himself, it is to spend the next seven months, according to Virgil, sitting on a crag by the side of the river Strymon, weeping and singing the song of his sorrow. For Ovid, this stage of mourning lasts three years, during which time he rejects the affection of all women, though many vie for his attention. Ovid adds the curious detail that it was Orpheus, at this period, who introduced to Thrace the practice of men loving boys.

And then something truly horrific happens. Suddenly one day, a band of Thracian women, ecstatic followers of Dionysus, rush upon Orpheus in a Bacchic frenzy. Enraged by either his abandonment of the love of women or his excessive love for the dead Eurydice, they descend upon him and tear him apart, in what must surely be in some way a reenactment of the primitive dismemberment of Dionysus/Zagreus through which a reborn god emerged.

I am not a follower of the sacred mysteries, and I can only shudder at the violent death of Orpheus, at the thought of his dismembered limbs and organs scattered on the bloody ground, of his severed head and his lyre thrown into the river Hebrus, where they float out to sea, perhaps to reach the island of Lesbos. Let me take some small comfort that there, his head and lyre will be recovered and a shrine built in his name. But let me quickly retreat to the more comforting thought that in the Underworld, Orpheus is whole once more and is reunited forever with his beloved Eurydice.

21

Alcestis and Admetus: Lost Love

There is a nightmarish parlor game I suspect we have all played at some point in our lives, whether with ourselves or with others, and whether we admit to it or not. We are put in the position of having to choose one person to die so that another may live. Perhaps the choice is between a brilliant and world-renowned artist on the one hand—the creator of great and humane masterpieces, but a nasty and vindictive individual in real life—and an otherwise anonymous individual on the other hand, someone of humble standing and no particular accomplishment, but who has touched with kindness the lives of anyone with whom he has come into contact. Can one life be valued over the other? Which of these two is to be spared?

In an even worse fantasy, we are forced to sacrifice someone we know and love, perhaps even a member of our own family, so that another person we hold dear may live. This is a Sophie's choice, and one almost too dreadful to consider. But it is a choice that in myth Admetus, king of Pherae in Thessaly, actually did make, and with one rather ugly twist: The life he chose to save at the expense of another was his own. That things turned out well for him in the end is perhaps a telling marker of the distance between the ancient world and our own.

Let me start from the beginning. Asclepius, the God of Medicine and Healing, was the son of Apollo. Because he was able to bring people back from the brink of death or beyond, Hades, King of the Underworld, grew fearful and asked Zeus to put an end to the upstart's activities. Zeus smote him with a thunderbolt manufactured by the Cyclopes who lived under Mount Aetna. Apollo, distraught at the death of his son, took vengeance on the Cyclopes, for which Zeus punished him in turn: Apollo would be banished from Olympus for a year, during which time he would take on a lowly identity and work in service to a mortal. And it is under these circumstances that he came to the door of Admetus's palace as a stranger, was warmly welcomed, and was given the responsibility for tending the king's herds.

Shortly after this, Pelias, king of Iolcus, sought a husband for his daughter Alcestis. As so often seems the case in these myths, the competition for the princess's hand was intense, and her father narrowed down the field by setting impossible-seeming conditions: Whichever suitor could yoke a lion and a boar to a chariot would win the bride. Did Pelias really want to marry off his daughter, one wonders. But never mind. In continued gratitude for the way he had been treated during his period of servitude, Apollo equipped a chariot with the required team of mismatched and wild beasts for Admetus, who was able to ride away with Alcestis as his wife.

Whether it was because he failed to make proper sacrifice to Artemis after the wedding or more simply because the Fates had determined that it would soon be time to cut the thread of his life, the day of Admetus's death approached. Apollo, now restored to glory but still grateful for the king's earlier hospitality and protection, got the Fates drunk and negotiated an extension with them. He presented the terms of the deal to the beneficiary: If Admetus could convince someone else to die in his place on the appointed day, his life would be spared. The king agreed without a moment's hesitation and then discovered that it is not only kings who cling to life.

Soldiers are willing to lay down their lives in battle for their country, but none seem to have volunteered to save their king in time of peace. Admetus turned next to his aged mother and father. Surely no parent could allow a child to die. Surely either mother or father would give up that small remainder left of a life well lived so that their only son might have the chance to reach old age as well. But they refused. Admetus reviled them for their selfishness, while they wondered how he could be foolish or presumptuous enough to think that life is any less precious to the elderly than to the young; if anything, every day is prized all the more highly when one has a sense of how few days may be left.

And then someone did come forward who was willing to die prematurely so that Admetus might live. It was Alcestis, the wife he had won with the help of Apollo.

The fullest version of the story that survives is in the play by Euripides that bears Alcestis's name. The action unfolds on the newly determined day of Alcestis's death, and we first encounter her as seen through the eyes of her maid, who reports on the queen's actions. On what she senses is the final morning of her life, Alcestis solemnly dresses and puts on her finest jewels, presumably the treasure with which she expects to be buried. She then goes to embrace her small son and daughter. She wishes for them the long life that she will not have, prosperous adulthoods and happy marriages she will never get to witness. She behaves, as we would say, like a real lady, and the maid next describes how all the servants in the household came forward one by one, weeping for their mistress, and how Alcestis had kind and gracious words for each, no matter how low their standing. Admetus is now at the side of his dying wife, we hear, holding her in his arms and begging her not to forsake him. But that is not possible, for the bargain with the Fates has been made, and of course it is Admetus who has agreed to it. Alcestis's strength is ebbing and her remaining hours are few. She asks to be carried outside, so that she may see the sun for one last time.

Alcestis is brought out to the forecourt of the palace on a litter, shadowed in the play by a personification of Death. She utters her final wish—that Admetus never remarry, not for the sake of remaining faithful to her memory, but so that her daughter may not be neglected or even abused by a resentful stepmother. She explains why it is she chose to die in Admetus's place:

> I put you first, and at the price of my own life
> Made certain you would live and see the daylight.
> So I die, who did not have to die, because of you.
> I could have taken any man in Thessaly
> I wished and lived in queenly state here in this house,
> But since I did not wish to live bereft of you
> And with our children fatherless, I did not spare
> My youth, although I had so much to live for.
> —Euripides, *Alcestis*

Does Alcestis love Admetus more than life itself, or does she sacrifice herself out of a sense of duty to him and the institution of marriage? I'm not sure. Elsewhere in the play, she curses the conjugal bed as the source of her unhappiness and declares that she will never again say that marriage brings more pleasure than pain. What is clear is that Admetus has accepted from her a sacrifice he would not have made in return. He has valued his life above all others', including hers. As she is dying he weeps and moans that had he Orpheus's voice, he would follow her down to the Underworld and bring her back successfully. But of course he is no poet or singer.

After she dies, he does seem to have a moment of tragic recognition, when he realizes how bad he must look to the outside world: He has gained no honor by asking his parents to die in his place, and certainly none by allowing his wife to do so. Which does he mourn more, the loss of his wife and the mother of his children, or the compromise of his reputation? It is the latter, I think, and to us it is not a pretty scene to witness.

> "You were a stranger to sorrow: therefore Fate has cursed you."
> —Admetus, from Euripides, *Alcestis*

And yet, Alcestis is brought back to life through Admetus's actions in the end.

Just as he had earlier been rewarded by the god Apollo for his kindness to strangers, so does he benefit once more from the actions of another to whom he has extended his hospitality. In the ancient Greek world, few relationships were more honored than that between host and guest, and if Admetus has been a careless and incomparably selfish husband, he has always been of unsurpassed generosity to visitors. On the very day of Alcestis's death and funeral, the hero Heracles, en route to perform one of his twelve labors, comes to the door of his old friend Admetus, seeking shelter for the night. Admetus is as accommodating a host as he has always been in the past, taking pains to shield his guest on this occasion from knowledge of the grief that has descended upon the house just hours before. But one of the servants lets slip to the muscular guest that the mistress of the house has died, and Heracles resolves to make matters right. He goes to the grave site where the figure of Death is on the point of escorting Alcestis to the Underworld. Heracles pummels Death into submission and frees Alcestis from his grasp. What Orpheus could not in the end accomplish by song or poetry, Heracles achieves with brute force.

At the end of Euripides's play, Heracles restores a living Alcestis to an unbelieving Admetus. It is a scene that seems to anticipate the ending of Shakespeare's *Winter's Tale*, where Hermione, long thought dead, is restored to her still-grieving husband, Leontes. But unlike Hermione, Alcestis doesn't say a word. How to explain her silence? Heracles says that having been brought back from death, Alcestis will not be able to speak until she has completed a three-day period of purification, and I'm sure this seemed plausible to the ancient Greeks. Modern scholars might say that Alcestis cannot speak because beneath their dramatic masks, the characters of Heracles and Alcestis, who have not appeared on stage together until this moment, were played by a single actor; it is now someone else acting as a mute stand-in for Alcestis, wearing her mask and costume. And that may also

111

be right. But I know that were I Alcestis, I would simply be too angry or depressed to speak to the man whose selfishness had very nearly killed me. Admetus may be a fine host indeed, but from the modern perspective I see only the manipulative and abusive husband.

22

Cephalus and Procris: Toxic Love

We all know couples who claim to love each other, and maybe do, but who separate nonetheless, as maybe they should, then reunite, as perhaps they should not. Their lives are filled with betrayals and counter-betrayals, and sometimes the ending is tragic. Cephalus and Procris are one such pair, and I think it's not accidental that their story comes down to us with enough twists and turns and bickering variants that in the end we don't know whom or what to believe. But we do know that things went terribly wrong.

It all started off well enough. Cephalos was the son of Deion, ruler of Phocis, and Procris was the daughter of Erechtheus, one of the founders of Athens. We can be sure that they were a very handsome couple and that they seemed very much in love as well. Every version of the story agrees that they were both avid hunters—it is good for a couple to share hobbies and pastimes. And in at least one account, they took a vow to remain true to each other always and never in their lives to sleep with any other partner. In another, it is hinted that the gods noticed their too great happiness and chose to put it to the test.

One morning—it was two months after the wedding, according to one account—Cephalus went hunting by himself, as he sometimes did. Eos, or Aurora, the Goddess of the Dawn, saw him, was enraptured, and wanted him for her own. She attempted to seduce him, but when he told her of his vow to remain faithful to Procris, she backed off, saying that she would not ask him to break such an oath unless Procris had done so first. She devised a stratagem to her advantage: She would change Cephalus's appearance so totally that he could come to Procris as a stranger, and one laden with gifts. If, in this guise and with these presents, he could persuade her to sleep with him, he would know that in principle, at least, Procris was unfaithful and Aurora could pursue the affair with a clear conscience.

Unless things happened somewhat differently. Perhaps, as another version has it, the goddess actually abducted him, carried him off, and held him against his will, maybe even for a period of years. If Cephalus's own words are to be believed (or at least, the words put into his mouth by Ovid in the *Metamorphoses*), the whole time he was with Aurora he could think and talk of nothing but the bride from whom he was so cruelly separated. He remained true to her and pined away, except that according to other sources, he somehow managed to sire one, two, maybe three children by the goddess. Be that as it may, eventually Aurora tired of hearing about her lover's wife and gave him his walking papers, but not before uttering, in either anger or frustration, that he could have his Procris but would rue the day he had ever met her.

Cephalus's reaction to this is troubling for what it may tell us about his character. Not for a moment does he attribute Aurora's words to jealousy or vindictiveness. Rather, they immediately plant a seed of suspicion in his mind. Is the goddess hinting that Procris has been unfaithful in his absence? Does she have some information that he does not? Betrayal would be against Procris's nature as he thought he knew it, but he has, after all, been gone a long time, and she is very beautiful and naïve. She must have been subjected to many temptations. In this account it is not Aurora who proposes to alter the appearance of Cephalus so that he may enter Athens unrecognized and try to prove his wife unchaste; it is Cephalus himself who returns to the goddess to ask that she give him the means by which to test his wife's virtue.

> "Go, ungrateful mortal, keep your wife, whom, if I am not much mistaken, you will one day be very sorry you ever saw again."
> —Aurora, from Thomas Bulfinch, *Bulfinch's Mythology*

And so it may have occurred that having been set up to test Procris's chastity oath by Aurora, Cephalus returned home after a brief absence in the guise of a stranger, tempted his wife with the gifts he carried, and easily seduced her.

Or perhaps, having been long absent and tormented by uncertainty, Cephalus returned to Athens and found his house in surprisingly good order, save for the prevailing grief over the loss of its master. With much difficulty and much deceit, he managed to gain an audience with Procris, the mistress of the house, who had isolated herself since the disappearance of her husband. She was more beautiful than ever. In his disguise, he made advances and was repeatedly rebuffed. Everything in her demeanor indicated that his suspicions had been misplaced. Were he not in the grip of an Othello-like jealousy, he would have walked away, convinced of her virtue. Instead he pressed on, almost self-destructively, as if wanting to assure his own unhappiness. Finally, after he had persisted and cajoled and promised her immense treasure should she relent, he managed to break down her resistance. At the moment she said she would sleep with him, he unmasked himself and declared her a faithless traitor to his love. Of course, he had to work exceptionally hard to get her to this point.

Or perhaps, as yet another version has it, the young bridegroom Cephalus never attracted the attention of Aurora, was never spirited away, and never tried to tempt his wife to infidelity at all. Perhaps she was in fact unfaithful nearly from the start. It was a stranger named Pteleon who seduced her, and who got into her bed by offering her the gift of a golden diadem. And Cephalus caught her in the act of committing adultery and was devastated by the betrayal.

However it happened—and there are versions of the myth that attest to all three scenarios—Procris fled Athens in shame. If you are inclined to think her promiscuous, you will follow her to Crete, where she took up residence at the court of King Minos. In him she had met her match in infidelity. In fact Pasiphaë, the wife of Minos, had previously grown so tired of his philandering that she had placed him under a curse: His semen was infused with venomous snakes, scorpions, and woodlice, so that any woman with whom he had intercourse would be immediately poisoned and die. Notwithstanding, Minos tried to seduce Procris. She was aware of the potentially fatal consequences, but was in possession of a secret antidote. She would sleep with Minos and lift the curse in exchange for two treasures in his possession: a hunting dog of rare ability and a javelin that always magically hit its mark. He readily agreed.

Once more, then, Procris offered sexual favors in return for merchandise. The exchange successfully made and fearing the wrath of Pasiphaë, Procris returned to Athens and Cephalus, with hound and javelin in tow. (And in case you are wondering how she cured Minos of his affliction and lived to tell the tale, the ancient grammarian Antoninus Liberalis tells us that she lined her vagina with a sheep's bladder, then tossed it away after intercourse, filled with his venomous ejaculate. This is fanciful, of course, but it is also the earliest account I know of someone safeguarding against infection by a sexually transmitted disease through use of a contraceptive, in this case a female condom.)

But perhaps Procris was neither mercenary nor sexually rapacious. Perhaps having been mistrusted and deceived by her husband, a virtuous Procris forsook the society of men and went off to join the company of the virgin Diana, the Goddess of the Hunt, with whom she remained until a contrite and miserable Cephalus sought her out, begged her forgiveness, and pleaded that she come back home. She relented, bearing with her two parting gifts from the goddess, once again, the hound and the javelin that would never miss its mark.

Or perhaps Procris had sought out Diana and been turned away, for the goddess allows only virgins in her cohort. But then Procris told the goddess her lamentable story, how at the instigation of Aurora, her own husband had manipulated her into committing what was, in all but a technical sense, adultery. Perhaps Diana then took pity on her and gave Procris the hound and the magic javelin, telling her to go off to compete with Cephalus in a hunt. Armed in this way she would humiliate and triumph over him. But now it is Procris who, at a goddess's insistence, disguises herself with intent to deceive. At Diana's bidding, Procris's hair is cut short as a boy's and she is dressed in male clothing. Her appearance so altered, she is able to return to Athens and challenge Cephalus to a hunting contest without his ever guessing her true identity.

As predicted, Procris, cross-dressed as a youth, easily triumphed. Recognizing the advantage that the hound and the marvelous javelin had given in the contest, Cephalus tried to buy both from the young stranger. She refused and he upped the ante: If only she would hand them over, he would share his throne with the mysterious youth. But Procris demurred still. Her identity still undiscovered, she said she would give up the dog and the spear only in return for sex with Cephalus. He unflinchingly agreed.

Now, the problems here are several, I would say. By taking on the role of deceiver, Procris has abandoned the moral high ground. By allowing himself to be so entrapped, Cephalus has shown himself just as incapable of keeping any fidelity oath as his wife. And if I am reading this correctly, in his avidity for the hound and the spear, he has agreed to sexual terms that would make him an object of scorn in the ancient world. It is not that he is willing to have sex with another man as the price for gaining these things; as we know, the Greeks and the Romans saw no opprobrium in same-sex male relations. But it is always the older man who must be the instigator and the active partner, and Cephalus has been propositioned by a youth and seems ready to cede the dominant sexual role to him. That is what would have been considered deeply shameful. And so they retire to the bedroom, and as she removes her clothing,

Procris reveals herself to be both a woman and the long-lost wife. Cephalus's infidelity is no infidelity, but his humiliation is real.

And now the story moves to its tragic end. At its simplest, a reunited Cephalus and Procris go out hunting together one day and are momentarily separated. As she is chasing something in the brush, he catches sight of the movement and mistakes her for wild game. He throws the javelin that never misses its mark and kills her instantly. But it is another version of events that seems truer to the spirit of the sad and tawdry story that this has become. After their betrayals and counter-betrayals, Cephalus and Procris are to all appearances happily reunited. And yet the relationship has been irrevocably poisoned by mistrust and deceit. As had been the case early in their marriage, it is once more Cephalus's habit to go off every morning to hunt in solitude in the woods.

Perhaps, after his exertions, and covered in perspiration, he retreats to the shade of a tree and calls out to the cool breeze, begging it to come and touch his skin to bring him comfort. And perhaps someone passing by overhears this soliloquy, thinks Cephalus is speaking to a lover, and reports the clandestine affair to Procris. Or perhaps Procris needs to hear no tales but is suspicious on her own that the real reason Cephalus retreats to the woods each morning is for a tryst with his old mistress, the goddess Aurora. Either way, an untrusting Procris follows Cephalus one day in secret and hides behind the bushes to spy on him. There is no lover, and when she stirs to approach her husband or to leave the scene, he throws the javelin that never misses its target and mortally wounds her. He reaches her as she lies dying and begs her never to leave. She bids him never to remarry. She expires in his arms.

Does it make any sense to ask which of the two, Procris or Cephalus, was the truer lover? Better, perhaps, to ask which member of this golden, toxic couple was the less false and to hope that we may all be less manipulative and more trusting than either.

23

Acontius and Cydippe: A Marriage of True Minds

We know from the archaeological records that the ancient Greeks and Romans wrote on many different kinds of surfaces. Inscriptions have come down to us carved into stone or painted onto pottery. Texts were preserved on scrolls of paperlike papyrus, and individuals kept notes or wrote letters on small tablets of wood or clay. And if we were to go by the additional evidence of myths, we might be tempted to add one more medium to the list: apples hurled through the air.

Now, I don't really believe that messages were sent back and forth written on pieces of fruit, but you will recall that it was an inscribed apple, thrown into a gathering of gods and goddesses, that precipitated the Judgment of Paris and the Trojan War. And it is also an oath written on an apple and tossed into the Temple of Artemis at Delos that lies at the heart of the story of Acontius and Cydippe. This may not be one of the better-known myths, but I find it one of the most charming. Love, in the Greek and Roman myths, is a powerful and usually irrational force, as we have seen, and I've been surprised as I've gathered materials for this book how often it ends badly. The tale of Acontius and Cydippe, though, is one of the very few that has the shape of a romantic comedy of the sort familiar to us from Shakespeare's plays and Hollywood movies alike.

You know the contours of the story: Two people meet, and either they take an instant dislike to one another or one is interested and the other resists. They separate, and often an unsuitable prospect arrives on the scene for one of them. The wrong marriage must somehow be averted so that the right couple—our hero and heroine—can recognize that they are meant for each other and wed in the end. Often a serious, and in itself non-comic, crisis of some sort—banishment, disease, even the death of a loved one—serves as a catalyst to the resolution. Boy meets girl, boy loses girl, boy gets girl.

The fullest version of this particular boy/girl story to have come down to us is once again from Ovid, who ends his *Heroides* with a pair of letters between Cydippe and Acontius, at a point at which they are not quite yet reconciled to be lovers. Ovid had it in turn from the Alexandrian writer Callimachus, whose poem "Cydippe" has survived only in fragments. Other poets too make passing use of the story in their works. We can piece it together as follows:

Acontius was a handsome and well-born youth from Ceos who had come to Delos, the island sacred to Artemis (the Roman Diana), to celebrate her annual festival. Entering the temple precincts one day, he espied the beautiful and equally high-born Cydippe, who had come with her mother, from either Athens or Naxos (Callimachus and Ovid disagree on this point) for the same purpose. While her mother was occupied making a sacrifice at the altar of the goddess, Cydippe waited, strolling along the temple colonnades with the ubiquitous nurse. For Acontius it was love at first sight. He grabbed an apple, inscribed something into it, and threw it in their direction. The apple landed at the feet of the nurse, who picked it up and handed it to her mistress. She in turn held it up and read aloud the words the young man had written: "I swear by the sanctuary of Diana to marry Acontius." As an opening gambit, it is a miserable failure. Cydippe disposes of the apple in annoyance and continues on her way. The goddess, however, has heard and takes notice.

The festival ended, Cydippe and her mother return home without any further thought given to the curious incident of the apple in the temple. Acontius, for his part, sails back to Ceos confident that he will somehow be hearing from them. He waits to see what happens next. But when, within a short span, it is time for the father of Cydippe to choose a husband for her, he selects a suitable young man who is not Acontius.

The plans for the marriage proceed without incident until the night before the wedding. It is the custom of Naxos for the betrothed couple to sleep in the same bed, chastely it seems, in a rite that is somehow meant to honor the union of Zeus and Hera. Cydippe becomes suddenly and gravely ill. Callimachus offers clinical details that must have been more meaningful to his original audience than they are to us. She has been afflicted with what some incorrectly call the sacred disease (this may refer to epilepsy), he writes; it is the illness that we send away onto mountain goats (I have no idea what this could possibly mean). In Ovid, Cydippe herself describes her symptoms: She has lost all color, she is fevered and has grown terribly weak, she can barely lift her limbs, and the wasted flesh hangs from her bones. She is not expected to live. When it seems likely that the torches that had been prepared to light her wedding will find new and mournful use at her funeral, the engagement is called off and the chosen bridegroom withdraws. And just as suddenly as she had fallen ill, and rather more miraculously, Cydippe is restored to health and beauty.

An appropriate interval is allowed to pass, and Cydippe's father chooses another husband for her. Once again, elaborate wedding preparations are made, and once again all goes well until the night before the nuptials. Then once again, on the eve of her marriage, Cydippe is struck down by the very same illness. This time surely she cannot survive. As before, the wedding is canceled and the prospective bridegroom retreats in sorrow. And as before, Cydippe suddenly and fully recovers.

It is when this same sequence of events is occurring for a third time, with Cydippe betrothed to yet another man and once more gravely ill, that the story reaches its resolution. Were she the subject of a modern medical case study, Cydippe would certainly have been diagnosed with some sort of severe psychopathological disorder by now, but that is not at all where the narrative takes us. Word has reached Acontius back in Ceos of Cydippe's three aborted marriages, and he decides the time has finally come to present himself in person.

Cydippe's father, meanwhile, has gone to consult the Oracle at Delphi over the cause of his daughter's three life-threatening illnesses. The Oracle responds that Cydippe is being punished for having perjured herself before Artemis. He returns home, the incident of the apple is revealed, and Acontius and Cydippe are united as a couple, as was meant to be.

It is true that Acontius is not very good at wooing. He has never addressed Cydippe directly, never actually tried to woo her or win her over by persuasion.

"Diana herself wishes you guiltless, and strives to hinder you from running into perjury; she desires, that with faith unstained, you may avoid giving offence. Hence, as often as you are in danger of being perfidious, the Goddess prevents the fatal crime."

—Acontius, from Ovid, *The Epistles of Ovid*

Cydippe points this out in the letter Ovid allows her to write to Acontius. Rather, he took her unawares and tricked her into uttering the words of the oath in the temple of Artemis. You might say, as Cydippe herself does in the *Heroides*, that she was merely caught by a technicality: If she was simply reading the words without intending their meaning, the words are hollow and the oath should in no way be binding. She is a shrewd heroine and is making a smart case here. And I love her for this.

In his own defense, Acontius points out that unwanted and one sided as his attentions might have been, he never resorted to force—as, for example, Paris did when he seized Helen—but rather sought to win Cydippe by wit. And his wit is what I love about him in turn. When you think about it, he not only tricked Cydippe with his apple toss, but he simultaneously tricked the goddess Artemis, too. It is not Acontius who is doing Artemis's bidding, but Artemis who has been maneuvered into doing his. This is quite extraordinary! Can you think of another myth in which it is not a mortal who is caught up in the schemes of the gods but vice versa? I can't.

I have a smile on my face when I think of Cydippe relenting in the end and recognizing that in Acontius she has met her match in every way. Perhaps I get carried away when I start thinking of them as ancient versions of Shakespeare's Beatrice and Benedict or Hollywood's Hepburn and Tracy. Perhaps not.

24

Ceyx and Alcyone:
Calming the Waters

There is a brief anecdote told by the writer we know as the Pseudo-Apollodorus about King Ceyx and his wife, Alcyone. The two had taken to calling one another Zeus and Hera, and when this came to the attention of Zeus himself, he transformed them into seabirds to punish them for their arrogance. Apollodorus's source seems to be a lost text by the important archaic Greek poet Hesiod, and he is certainly not an authority to dismiss lightly. But others tell of Ceyx and Alcyone as well, and I suspect they would have found this particular version highly implausible. Not because a man and a woman are turned into birds, mind you. Things like that happen in myth often enough. Rather, it is because Ceyx and Alcyone would never have chosen these particular pet names. Zeus and Hera, Roman Jupiter and Juno, never seem to like or trust each other very much. Ceyx and Alcyone were a husband and wife deeply in love.

Ceyx was ruler of Trachis and son of Eosphorus, or Lucifer, the morning star. His brother Daedalion, we learn, was of a bellicose and predatory temperament, but Ceyx is peaceful by nature, pious and just. He is welcoming of strangers—an attribute, as we have seen, of the highest importance in the Greek and Roman world—and a loving and solicitous husband, not at all a given in these societies. Alcyone is the daughter of Aeolus, the Keeper of the

Winds, and the equal of her husband in every possible way, including the depth and kindness of her love.

All within a short span of time, things become unsettled. Daedalion's daughter Chione is impregnated by both Apollo and Hermes and slain by Artemis for her vainglory; Daedalion himself is metamorphosed into a hawk; and a ravenous wolf of more than natural strength and ferocity comes out of the swamp to decimate the herds of Peleus, a royal visitor to Trachis, and is stopped only when he is turned to stone. Feeling anxious about this chain of events, as well he might, Ceyx resolves to consult the oracle at Claros on the coast of Asia Minor, and he informs Alcyone of his decision.

She is terrified. Even were she not Aeolus's daughter with direct experience of the violent unpredictability of the winds, she would know enough of the perils of sea travel to give her reasons for trying to dissuade her husband from hazarding the voyage. She has far too often seen the shattered wreckage of ships washing ashore; she has far too often passed the empty tombs constructed on land for sailors lost at sea. If he must go, she begs him to take her along. At best she would see that he was safe and well and thus would be spared her dreadful imaginings of unknown dangers. At worst, if his ship were to go down, she would be there with him to share his fate.

Ceyx does not dismiss her concerns as unreasonable. Both he and his wife understand far better than Hero or Leander ever did the dangers of the sea. But neither does he change his plans, for he fears Trachis is in trouble and the oracle must be consulted. This he promises, however: If the fates allow, he will return to Alcyone before two months have passed.

The fullest version of the myth that we have is once again in Ovid's *Metamorphoses*; in fact, as has

> "Every delay will seem long to us indeed, but I swear to you by my father's light, to return to you as long as the fates allow it, before the moon has twice completed her circle."
> —Ceyx, from Ovid, *Metamorphoses*, 11

been noticed, the story of Ceyx and Alcyone is actually the longest sustained narrative in all of Ovid's kaleidoscopic poem. I can't imagine a richer, more concrete, or more heartbreaking account of what happens next than his. Ovid takes Ceyx and Alcyone down to the harbor where they say their good-byes. He then follows Alcyone's gaze as she focuses first on Ceyx standing on the deck of the ship, then on the ship itself as it recedes further into the distance, growing ever smaller and more indistinct until it is not even a speck on the horizon.

And Ovid conjures up, in horrifying detail, the dreadful storm that lays siege to the ship when it is halfway to Claros, and the final moments of the doomed sailors. One weeps uncontrollably, while another stands in catatonic silence. Another still calls out in vain to the gods for help, while others cry out for their homes or children, their brothers or fathers. But Ceyx thinks only of Alcyone, of his love for her, of how he would wish to see her once more, but also of the comfort he can take in knowing that she is safe ashore. As the ship breaks apart, he clings to a piece of flotsam tossing in the sea, repeating Alcyone's name over and over and praying, in that small bit of time remaining before he is swallowed by the waters, that the waves may carry his body back to Alcyone and that her loving hands may prepare him for his tomb.

Like Penelope at home in Ithaca awaiting the return of her absent Odysseus, Alcyone back in Trachis occupies herself with weaving. She is crafting the garments that she hopes she and Ceyx will wear when they are at last reunited. She counts down each passing night and prays to Juno that Ceyx may be kept from harm, that he will return, and that he will never love any woman more than he loves her. And that last is the only part of the prayer that can ever be granted.

In Ovid's account, Juno can no longer bear to hear Alcyone's prayers, though he does not specify why. Is it because knowing that the pleas for Ceyx's safe return are in vain, they have become merely tiresome to her? Or is it because they are too painfully heartrending to hear? I would like to believe the latter, but Juno has never been the most sympathetic of goddesses. In any event, she goes down to the cave of Sleep and arranges for his henchman Morpheus to appear to Alcyone in a dream in the shape of the drowned Ceyx and to inform her of the fact and circumstances of Ceyx's death. Many have puzzled over the oddity that it is not the true shade of Ceyx but a perfect imposter, who nevertheless reveals the truth to Alcyone even as he lies repeatedly to her about his identity. She awakens with a start, certain in the knowledge that Ceyx is no more, and that with his death, a large part of her died as well.

There is a short philosophical dialogue called the "Halcyon"—sometimes attributed to Plato and sometimes to the second-century-CE Greek writer Lucian, though it was certainly written by neither—that offers one version of what happens next: They say that the daughter of the Greek Aeolus is lamenting her young husband, Ceyx the Trachinian, son of the morning star, handsome child of a handsome father. Out of longing for his love, through a god's will she becomes winged like a bird and flies about all over the sea seeking him; but though she wanders all over the world, she is not able to find him.

As Hesiod and the Pseudo-Apollodorus had it, then, Alcyone is metamorphosed into a bird, though not as punishment. And while no widow has ever been turned into a seabird by her sorrow, there is an undeniable emotional reality to this ending that I can well understand. Having lost the one being she loved above all others, the single person by whom she felt herself completed, Alcyone feels changed and somehow permanently diminished. She will never emerge from her grief and will spend the rest of her days in a state of perpetual, perhaps even pathological, mourning, ungrounded and adrift, forever looking to find that which can never be recovered.

But I prefer Ovid's ending.

As soon as morning comes, Alcyone goes down to the shore, to that very spot from which Ceyx had set sail and from which she watched as he grew smaller and smaller until he had disappeared into the distance, moving forever out of her sight. And now something truly miraculous happens. Far out to sea, she can discern a small speck floating in the water. It is coming toward land, bobbing in the waves, and as it comes more fully into view, as it comes nearer and nearer, she is able to make out that it is a man, a corpse, the body of a drowned mariner, that of Ceyx himself. She rushes along the jetty, tearing her hair in grief, and hurls herself into the sea in his direction.

But unlike Hero, leaping from her tower to the washed-up body of Leander, she does not jump to her death. She seems to be carried on the air. She sprouts feathers and wings and is transformed into a bird, but a bird now flying directly toward her love. She alights on his body and cradles him with her soft downy feathers. As she tries to kiss him, no longer with her lips but with her bill, his face seems to rise up to meet hers.

> "Though it was amazing that she could do so, she leapt onto it: she flew, and, beating the soft air on new-found wings, a sorrowing bird, she skimmed the surface of the waves. As she flew, her plaintive voice came from a slender beak, like someone grieving and full of sorrows. When she reached the mute and bloodless corpse, she clasped the dear limbs with her new wings and kissed the cold lips in vain with her hard beak."
> —Ovid, *Metamorphoses*, 11

It is not merely the movement of the waves, for the gods have taken pity on their love and have actually restored him to life, not falsely, as they had Protesilaus, but not as he had been either. He too is now transformed. Once man and wife, Ceyx and Alcyone are now the halcyons, mythical kingfishers that live on the surface of the sea and remain inseparable, mated for life. And once every winter, for the span of just one week, the seas and the winds are calmed, so that Ceyx may brood on her floating nest and hatch her young. These are the halcyon days beloved by sailors.

It is not the case that the good are rewarded in this life, that those who love and act wisely and well will escape all misfortune. I am a great optimist, but trust me, I know this all too well. And if in this story Daedalion and Chione are appropriately punished for their pride or iniquity, and if elsewhere we can understand why Hero and Leander meet their doom, then it seems that Ceyx and Alcyone suffer sorrows that they never deserved. It is a fable, a fairy tale, I realize—but still, I take great comfort that in the end their goodness and their love overcome everything, even death.

25

Baucis and Philemon: Love at the End

Many cultures tell the story of a great flood that engulfs and eradicates all but a remnant of the earth's population. A god or gods, despairing at the evil that has taken hold of humankind, cause the waters of the world to rise, sparing only the very few virtuous individuals to be found, men and women of extraordinary goodness who are now charged with the task of rebuilding civilization not as it was but as it was meant to be. For most of us, the story of Noah and his ark is no doubt the most familiar version by far. But I wish to conclude with one version of the flood myth as the Greeks and the Romans told it, for I have come to think that it is also one of the most beautiful love stories of all. As far as we know, it appears first in the eighth book of Ovid's *Metamorphoses*.

Jupiter and Mercury came down once to the land of Phrygia, disguised as travelers begging for food and shelter. Now, the Greek and Roman gods often take on human appearance so that they may move among mortals unnoticed. Often they have mischief on their minds, and often sex. This time, they had neither. Wandering from house to house, the two gods simply knocked on doors, seeking hospitality. In our time, we would no doubt be suspicious of strangers asking for a meal and a bed for the night, but in the ancient world as we know, at least as the ancients themselves idealized it, few things were as sacred as the host-guest relationship. And yet, Ovid tells us, the two gods knocked on a thousand doors and were turned away from each. Finally, they reached the poor hut of an elderly couple, Baucis and Philemon. They alone invited the strangers in, and though they had very little, they shared everything— fruits and nuts, honey and cheese, a treasured bit of bacon hanging from the beam of the house. To start her cooking fire, old Baucis even had to pull some of the thatch off the roof for kindling.

Ovid doesn't dwell on the matter, but it is obvious that age has taken its toll on Baucis and Philemon. There is a tremor in the old lady's hands as she sets the table or props up one of its broken legs with a piece of broken pottery. When the two light upon the idea of catching their one barnyard animal, a goose, to serve as the main course of their guests' dinner, the bird outruns and exhausts them both. And though Ovid doesn't overstate it, at least not at first, it is clear that the couple love each other very much. Apparently childless, they have lived in that simple hut their whole married life. They have grown old together there, delighted in each other's company, and remained content in spite of their poverty. When Ovid tells us that we need not look for servants or masters in the household, for Baucis and Philemon were servants and masters both, we can imagine this as a joke they have tirelessly repeated over the years as they putter around their modest cottage. On how many occasions did Philemon honor his ladyship by offering up some cabbage leaves brought in from the garden? How often, in turn, did Baucis stew up an elegant pot of the same for the lord of the tiny manor? But at this moment, they had company, and without quibbling in the kitchen—indeed, with little apparent need for speech of any kind—the two, clearly unaccustomed to entertaining but fully attuned to each other, lay out the spread for their visitors.

And then, they both notice the same strange thing: No matter how much the guests drank of the poor wine set before them, the bowl remained filled. The explanation is forthcoming: "We are gods," Jupiter and Mercury declare— and they promptly state their intention of destroying by flood everyone who had turned them away. They take Philemon and Baucis to the summit of a hill, from which they can see the floodwaters rise and recede. Only the hut of Philemon and Baucis is spared, but before their eyes it is miraculously transformed into a glorious temple, its humble wooden supports made marble, its thatched roof turned to gold. Philemon and Baucis themselves become its priest and priestess—but they remain mortal.

Humble Philemon, who up until now, has asked for nothing, has one request of the gods: "Since my wife and I have been inseparable our whole lives, grant us that we both may die at the same hour, so that I may never see her tomb nor she my grave." And so it came to be. One day, as they stood before the temple, talking of their lives together, they are transformed before each other's eyes into trees. As the bark creeps up their bodies, they simultaneously bid each other farewell. But they are not separated; before the temple, Ovid tells us, there now stand a linden tree and an oak, their branches forever entwined.

When my husband died, my grief was tremendous, and not a day goes by that I do not wish that he were still by my side. But as deeply as I loved him, as fully as we shared our lives together and as unimaginable I thought a life without him would be, I could never have made the choice of Philemon and Baucis. Whatever the sorrow I feel, I also look forward to what each new day might bring. I have been so fortunate in the time that he has been gone to be able to travel to places I'd never been, to write, teach, and lecture, to see the birth of one grandchild and to watch as three others grow in the most extraordinary ways. I have met so many wonderful people, whose lives have enriched me with love and whose lives, I can only hope, I have enriched in some way, too. Still, I think, from time to time of a comment that a wise and dear old friend once made many years ago—that there can be no good end to a good marriage. The myth of Baucis and Philemon demonstrates otherwise. But their way could never be mine.

"They had charge of the temple while they lived: and when they were released by old age, and by the years, as they chanced to be standing by the sacred steps, discussing the subject of their deaths, Baucis saw Philomen put out leaves, and old Philemon saw Baucis put out leaves, and as the tops of the trees grew over their two faces, they exchanged words, while they still could, saying, in the same breath: 'Farewell, O dear companion,' as, in the same breath, the bark covered them, concealing their mouths."
—Ovid, *Metamorphoses*, 8

Reading Notes

Chapter 1: Tiresias: The Riddle of Pleasure and the Burden of Shame

Highlighted Themes
- A sense of shame regarding sex and sexuality
- The transgendered experience
- Perspectives of sexuality that cross gender lines.

Pivotal Questions
Do Tiresias's experiences with both genders give him particular insight to the experience of the opposite sex? Would his experiences as a woman have changed how he acted when he returned to being a man, or would being male again cause his previous patterns of behavior to reassert themselves?

Exploring Transgender Themes in Modern Art
A good place to start is *Orlando*, a 1928 novel by Virginia Woolf. An Elizabethan courtier is born a male but is eventually transformed into a female, living over several centuries and experiencing the rigid confines of womanhood in several distinct eras and locations. *Orlando* (1992), starring Tilda Swinton, is a good film adaptation of the book. A similarly gender-shifting Orlando character appears in the graphic novels *The League of Extraordinary Gentlemen: Black Dossier* (2003) and *The League of Extraordinary Gentlemen, Vol. III: Century* (2009) by Alan Moore.

Many films also mimic Tiresias's insights into sex, love, and relationships from a transgender or gender-switched experience. Here are a few: *Tootsie* (1982), starring Dustin Hoffman; *Switch* (1991), starring Ellen Barkin; *Boys Don't Cry* (1999), starring Hilary Swank; *Transamerica* (2005), starring Felicity Huffman; and *Albert Nobbs* (2011), starring Glenn Close.

Chapter 2: Phaedrus and Hippolytus: What Is This Thing Called Love?

Highlighted Themes
- Older women and younger men
- Obsessive, sexual lust versus celibacy
- Thwarted incestuous passion

Pivotal questions

In what ways do we still see older women with younger men as "tragic" in our culture? Why? Do we often view obsessive sexual desire as inevitably tragic? Also, how do we tend to view lifelong commitments to celibacy as unhealthy or unnatural? In what ways is our society of a conflicted mind about sex versus celibacy?

Why Phaedra Is So Often an Important Role for Women

The role of Phaedra is popular because of the major acting opportunity it brings to middle-aged female actors, who find that meaty, emotional roles are harder to come by as they age. To be able to portray a woman in her middle years as fully sexual and possessing sexual desire—with all of the emotional highs and lows that accompany sexual desires—is a sort of holy grail for female actors. Once they reach the age that they can effectively act such a role, there are fewer and fewer opportunities for them to show that they can rise to that challenge. So they rush headlong toward such parts in the event they become available. And the same can sometimes be said for middle-aged women sexually: They're very good at sex but often have fewer opportunities to engage sexually. And so there is a parallel between the actor and the text that can be very powerful. And tempting.

Chapter 3. Cupid and Psyche: Love Discovered

Highlighted Themes

- The union of the "soul" (psyche) and "desire" (eros)
- Facing great trials to commit to love
- The role of trust in love and commitment

Pivotal Questions

What role does trust play in Cupid and Psyche's relationship? Is it fair for Cupid to ask Psyche to trust blindly? In what ways might his request for trust be justified? While erotic desire, or "eros," is flamed by physical passion, at what point does the soul, or "psyche," need to be fed in a relationship? How might Psyche have matured or evolved through her trials for Eros? How might those trials have deepened her commitment to love and the outcome of the story? How might trials contribute to modern love and relationships?

Prominent Literary References

In his 1819 poem "Ode to Psyche," John Keats explores his devotion to love of the imagination, represented by Psyche. In Till We Have Faces (1956), C. S. Lewis retells the Cupid and Psyche myth from the point of view of a sister.

Similar Motifs in Folklore

Motifs we encounter in the Cupid and Psyche myth can be found in *Beauty and the Beast* (enchanted palace, a lover in disguise), Grimm's *Cinderella* (trials for love, jealous sisters, helpful animals), and Bulfinch's *The Age of Fable*, which includes his version of Cupid and Psyche.

Paintings

- *Psyche et L'Amour* by William-Adolphe Bouguereau (1889); view image at http://en.wikipedia.org/wiki/File:Psyche_et_ LAmour.jpg

Chapter 4. Leda and the Swan: *Ceci n'est pas un cygne*

Highlighted Themes

- Forbidden eroticism
- Violence and weakness
- Rape, seduction, and its outcomes

Pivotal Questions

Considering the fates of Leda's daughters, how might issues of rape, seduction, and sexual history be passed from parent to child? Contrast the treatment of Leda and the Swan in the paintings of Correggio, Michelangelo, Leonardo da Vinci, and Boucher to the depiction of the myth in Yeats's short poem. How have attitudes toward the myth changed over the years? How have attitudes toward rape or seduction changed over the years? In what ways have they stayed the same?

Prominent Literary References

William Butler Yeats's poem "Leda and the Swan" (1924) is a Petrarchan sonnet that uses some of the most powerful language in modern English to explore the violence and weakness in Leda's rape, as well as the great magnitude of the eventual outcome—the birth of Helen, who inadvertently causes the Trojan War.

Paintings

- *Leda with the Swan* by Antonio da Correggio (1531); http://en.wikipedia.org/wiki/File:Correggio.jpg
- *Leda and the Swan* by Michelangelo Buonarroti (early 1500s); http://commons.wikimedia.org/wiki/File:Michelangelo_ Buonarroti_-_Leda_and_the_Swan_-_WGA15527.jpg
- *Leda and the Swan*, copy by Cesare da Sesto after a lost original by Leonardo da Vinci (1515–1520); http://en.wikipedia.org/wiki/File:Leda_and_the_Swan_1505- 1510.jpg

- *Leda and the Swan* by Francois Boucher (1741);
  http://www.wikipaintings.org/en/francois-boucher/leda-and-
  the-swan-1741

Leda and the Swan

A sudden blow: the great wings beating still
Above the staggering girl, her thighs caressed
By the dark webs, her nape caught in his bill,
He holds her helpless breast upon his breast.

How can those terrified vague fingers push
The feathered glory from her loosening thighs?
And how can body, laid in that white rush,
But feel the strange heart beating where it lies?

A shudder in the loins engenders there
The broken wall, the burning roof and tower
And Agamemnon dead.
Being so caught up,

So mastered by the brute blood of the air
Did she put on his knowledge with his power
Before the indifferent beak could let her drop?

- William Butler Yeats

Chapter 5. Helen and Paris: Lust and War

Highlighted Themes
- Lust, vanity, and the destruction they can bring

Pivotal Questions
In what ways has our culture made beauty the first priority of attrac-
tiveness? Do we see people today who rush into relationships based on
surface value? How has our culture also associated beauty with destructive qualities?

Prominent Literary References
The Tragical History of the Life and Death of Doctor Faustus, by
Christopher Marlowe (1604), has a famous monologue. When Dr.
Faustus conjures the image of Helen of Troy, he says:

Was this the face that launch'd a thousand ships,
And burnt the topless towers of Ilium?

141

Sweet Helen, make me immortal with a kiss.
Her lips suck forth my soul: see where it flies!
Come, Helen, come, give me my soul again.
Here will I dwell, for heaven is in these lips,
And all is dross that is not Helena.
I will be Paris, and for love of thee,
Instead of Troy, shall Wittenberg be sack'd;
And I will combat with weak Menelaus,
And wear thy colours on my plumed crest;
Yea, I will wound Achilles in the heel,
And then return to Helen for a kiss.
O, thou art fairer than the evening air
Clad in the beauty of a thousand stars;
Brighter art thou than flaming Jupiter
When he appear'd to hapless Semele;
More lovely than the monarch of the sky
In wanton Arethusa's azur'd arms;
And none but thou shalt be my paramour!

This passage occurs in act 5 of *Dr. Faustus*, toward the end of his deal with the devil, Mephistopheles. Faustus is looking for any opportunity to keep death at bay and is hoping that the vision of Helen will save him with a kiss. In return, he'd be willing to destroy Wittenberg in much the same way Troy was destroyed. In this way, his bargaining with the power of beauty reveals his desperation and corruption.

Paintings
- *The Love of Helen and Paris* by Jacques-Louis David (1788); http://en.wikipedia.org/wiki/File:Helene_Paris_David.jpg
- *Helen on the Ramparts of Troy* by Gustave Moreau (late nineteenth century); http://en.wikipedia.org/wiki/File:Helen_Moreau.jpg

Chapter 6. Laodamia and Protesilaus: Casualties of War

Highlighted Themes
- Grief and loss, which are so destructive when one is unable to let go of a lost love
- The burden of war widows

Pivotal Questions
Laodamia sacrificed joy while her husband was away at battle and again after her husband died. In what ways are her sacrifices commendable? Is there a point at which Laodamia's grief and sacrifice go from

commendable to dangerous? In what ways does her devotion to Protesilaus show strength and in what ways does it show weakness? Is her willingness to give up her own life rather than live without her husband romantic or tragic?

Prominent Literary References

William Wordsworth's narrative poem "Laodamia" (1815) recites the events of Protesilaus's return from the underworld, his reunion with his grieving widow, and her lamentations and death when he returns to the underworld.

Paintings

- *Laodamia* by George William Joy (late nineteenth century); http://www.bbc.co.uk/arts/yourpaintings/paintings/laodamia-24884

Chapter 7. Hermaphroditus and Salmacis: Love Denied

Highlighted Themes

- Female domination versus emasculation
- Love denied for selfish desire

Pivotal Questions

Does our culture still have the same attitudes about a woman pursuing a man as implied in "Hermaphroditus and Salmacis"? What does the myth imply about a man who allows himself to be overpowered by a woman's will? How does modern romance have to navigate such courses between the will of men and that of women? How would we judge Salmacis's behavior by modern standards? And would we judge it the same for both men and women?

Prominent Literary References

"Hermaphroditus," Algernon Charles Swinburne's 1866 ekphrastic poem (meaning a work of art that comments on another work of art), was inspired by the sculpture *Sleeping Hermaphroditus*, also known as the *Borghese Hermaphroditus* (http://www.poemhunter.com/poem/hermaphroditus/). The poem explores the tension between male and female placed in one form—neither pleasing each other nor fighting each other. The male-female form is one of beauty and desire, but one ultimately frustrated by an inability to be all male or all female.

Sculpture

- *Sleeping Hermaphroditus* (Borghese Hermaphroditus) by Gian Lorenzo Bernini, part of the Borghese Collection at the Louvre, Paris; http://en.wikipedia.org/wiki/File:Hermafrodita_2.JPG

143

Paintings
- *The Nymph Salmacis and Hermaphroditus* by François-Joseph Navez (1829); http://en.wikipedia.org/wiki/File:NAVEZ_Francois_Joseph_The_Nymph_Salmacis_And_Hermaphroditus.jpg

Chapter 8. Narcissus: Love Unshared

Highlighted Themes
- Destructiveness of narcissistic love
- Limitations of self-involved love

Pivotal Questions
Narcissus, at the beginning, rejected all suitors in his single-minded pursuit of pride. Today, some might call single-minded pursuit of success "dedication." When could that be a good thing and when might it cross a line? At the end of his story, Narcissus wastes away, never to know the touch of that which he loves. In what way might narcissists today suffer the same fate?

Prominent Literary References
Fred Chappell's poem "Narcissus and Echo" (1985) is a playful but powerful characterization of Narcissus at the water. The last syllable or two of each line is echoed, creating a message from Echo as Narcissus wastes away.

Paintings
- *Echo and Narcissus* by John William Waterhouse (1903); http://commons.wikimedia.org/wiki/File:John_William_Waterhouse_-_Echo_and_Narcissus_-_Google_Art_Project.jpg
- *Narcissus* by Michelangelo Merisi Caravaggio (1595); http://commons.wikimedia.org/wiki/File:Narcissus-Caravaggio_(1594-96)_edited.jpg

Chapter 9. Iphis and Ianthe: Gender-Bending Love

Highlighted Themes
- Traditional restrictions placed on heteronormative love
- The fluidity of gender traits between men and women
- The capability of women to love one another, despite cultural pressures against it

Pivotal Questions
How have our views of lesbian love shifted over the centuries? Are there ways in which some views have not changed? How would you compare

the suffering of Iphis regarding her love for Ianthe and the pain modern transgender people might feel? Although the ending of the myth reinforces heteronormative relationships, is there something to be said for the idea that the gods were willing to switch Iphis's gender for his happiness?

Prominent Literary References

Gender identity is a popular device throughout literature up to the present day, both in serious works such as the film *Boys Don't Cry* (1999) and in the comedies of Shakespeare (*As You Like It* and *Twelfth Night*, for example). Romance novels are replete with heroines disguised as boys, but the theme is very rare in reverse. While often treated with little seriousness in comedies, the works still highlight the fluidity of gender traits between the sexes. Modern dramas, however, take the difficulties of gender reassignment and gender identity very seriously because of the pain that transgendered individuals still suffer in society.

Chapter 10. Danaë: Pure Gold

Highlighted Themes
- Purity in sexual pleasure
- Purity in conception and birth

Pivotal Questions
Because of Zeus's incorporeal nature during this liaison and Danaë's virginity and innocent character, what might this myth imply about the role of purity and worthiness in terms of sex and love?

Paintings
- *Danaë* by Alexandre Jacques Chantron (1891);
  http://en.wikipedia.org/wiki/File:Alexandre_Jacques_Chantron_(1891)_Danae.jpg
- *Danaë* by Gustav Klimt (1907);
  http://commons.wikimedia.org/wiki/File:Gustav_Klimt_010.jpg?fastcci_from=405595

Chapter 11. Pasiphaë and the Bull: Animal Lust

Pivotal Questions
In the context of this book, this chapter may be best viewed as a prologue to the following chapter, which is about Theseus and Ariadne. But is there any takeaway from the awful story of a woman forced, by the actions of a god and a man, to mate with a bull in the most humiliating fashion? What does it say that this is made to happen as a "punishment" inflicted by Poseidon on Midas, although it's Midas's wife who bears the brunt of the pain?

Chapter 12. Theseus and Ariadne: Seduced and Abandoned, Part I

Highlighted Themes
- Lovers rise and succeed when helpful equals
- Even successful lovers may face an unhappy ending

Pivotal Questions
Compare how the Labyrinth and the Minotaur came to be created versus how the Minotaur came to be defeated. What are the differences between Minos and Pasiphaë's relationship and Theseus and Ariadne's relationship on Crete? Does the relationship ending negate the successes of Theseus and Ariadne in your mind?

Prominent Cultural References
As Ariadne was considered the "keeper of the Labyrinth" in the Greek myths, her name is often associated with mazes or puzzle makers, as well as puzzle solvers. In Agatha Christie's Poirot series, the famous, fastidious detective has a friend, Ariadne Oliver, who occasionally assists him in investigating mysteries.

And in the acclaimed 2010 film *Inception*, directed by Christopher Nolan, Ariadne is a student of architecture who helps create the structures of the mental mazes people experience in their dreams.

Paintings
- *Ariadne and Theseus* by Niccolò Bambini (date unknown); http://commons.wikimedia.org/wiki/File:Bambini,_Niccolo_-_Ariadne_and_Theseus.jpg

Chapter 13. Dido and Aeneas: Seduced and Abandoned, Part II

Highlighted Themes
- Love among equals
- Obligations at odds with love
- The effect of the gods or fate on love

Pivotal Questions
Dido and Aeneas both had quests to achieve, of a sort. Dido was the leader of an emerging city and was responsible for the care and work of its citizens. Aeneas had a specific objective given to him by his parents to flee and find a new home for the survivors of Troy. How do Dido's and Aeneas's obligations make their romance more difficult? In modern romance, how do the careers and ambitions of each partner enhance the relationship or distract from the relationship?

The gods have great influence over the actions and feelings of Dido and Aeneas. Does fate, circumstance, or predestination have any effect on modern romance? Or does it all come down to the responsibility of each partner?

Prominent Literary References

Henry Purcell's English opera *Dido and Aeneas* (1689) is the most prominent cultural work based on this myth, other than the *Aeneid* itself. Christopher Marlowe's play *Dido, Queen of Carthage* is another one to note. Dido and Aeneas turn up as characters in several literary works involving Rome or the Trojan War, such as Aeneas in Shakespeare's *Troilus and Cressida*. In a modern context, Dido has become a representation of female leadership, alongside Cleopatra, in the classical world.

Paintings

- *Aeneas Tells Dido about the Fall of Troy*, Pierre-Narcisse Guérin (1815); http://en.wikipedia.org/wiki/File:Gu%C3%A9rin_%C3%89n%C3%A9e_racontant_%C3%A0_Didon_les_malheurs_de_la_ville_de_Troie_Louvre_5184.jpg
- *The Death of Dido*, Guercino (1631); http://en.wikipedia.org/wiki/File:Guercino_Morte_di_Didone.jpg

Chapter 14. Pygmalion and the Statue: The Art of Love or the Love of Art?

Highlighted Themes

- Creating or changing a person to suit ones own ideals
- Objectification versus loving a true person

Pivotal Questions

In the case of Pygmalion, his sculpting the perfect spouse worked out for him. In what ways do we allow ourselves to be "molded" for the sake of our lovers' preferences? In what ways do we resist it? How do we treat and respect our lovers as individuals and yet learn to come together and change for the sake of the relationship? Is there a line between the individual's will and desires and the needs and preferences of the couple?

A societal note: This myth is quite prevalent in our modern culture in a variety of ways. Movies and television are replete with the theme, as are modern plays (*The Shape of Things* [2001] by Neil LaBute and staple films such as *Pretty Woman* [1990]). It is also in our social discourse, as both women and men struggle with issues of objectification in our romantic and gender relations.

Prominent Literary References

There are innumerable poems and stories based on the Pygmalion tale. And even more have similar themes. The most prominent in the English language is probably George Bernard Shaw's play *Pygmalion*, which in turn inspired the stage musical *My Fair Lady*. In it, Henry Higgins is Pygmalion to Eliza Doolittle's "statue." At first, Eliza is willing to be molded and changed to suit her mentor, but at some point, she exerts her own will and makes decisions for herself. She was always a real person, but through her education with Higgins she rises to her own potential.

The flip side, of course, is that often the Pygmalions and the Higginses are surprised when their "creation" that they are sculpting comes to life and has a will of its own. Some modern references, such as Carol Ann Duffy's 1999 poem "Pygmalion's Bride," explore how some Pygmalions prefer their brides cold and as an object, rather than as women with their own wild desires. This theme runs through Pygmalion references as often as the transformative theme.

Paintings

- *Pygmalion and Galatea*, by Louis-Jean-François Lagrenée (1781); http://commons.wikimedia.org/wiki/File:Pygmalion_and_Galatea_(Lagren%C3%A9e).jpg
- *Pygmalion and Galatea* by Jean-Léon Gérôme (1890); http://www.wikipaintings.org/en/jean-leon-gerome/pygmalion-and-galatea-1

Chapter 15. Canace and Macareus: All in the Family, Part I *and* Chapter 16. Myrrha and Cinyras: All in the Family, Part II

Highlighted Themes

- Destructiveness of secrecy and incest
- Punishment of duplicity and incest

Pivotal Questions

In both stories of incest, how did the young women involved (Canace and Myrrha) rationalize their feelings and behavior? Do people rationalize their strongest feelings and most transgressive behaviors in love in the same fashion today?

The ultimate results for each of the young lovers in these stories were the same: death. But how were their ends also radically different from each other? Was Myrrha's punishment somehow softened in comparison to Canace's? If so, why?

Paintings

- *The Birth of Adonis* by Marcantonio Franceschini (1685); http://en.wikipedia.org/wiki/File:%27Birth_of_Adonis%27,_oil_on_copper_painting_by_Marcantonio_Franceschini,_c._1685-90,_Staatliche_Kunstsammlungen,_Dresden.jpg

Chapter 17. Venus and Adonis: Unexpected Changes

Highlighted Themes

- To hunt or be hunted in love

Pivotal Questions

Adonis seems highly focused on his passion for the hunt, to the exclusion of sexual activity that would tempt many heterosexual men. What reasons could there be for his disdain of Venus's propositions? Sexual orientation, obsessive focus on his hunting activity, sexual inexperience perhaps, or too young? Perhaps he's "just not that into her"? In today's world, are there similar reasons for the rejection of one person by another?

Prominent Literary References

"Venus and Adonis," the epic poem by William Shakespeare (1592), uses the basis of Ovid's tale to explore the various aspects of romantic and sexual love.

Paintings

- *The Awakening of Adonis* by John William Waterhouse (1899); http://www.wikipaintings.org/en/john-william-waterhouse/the-awakening-of-adonis-1899
- *Venus und Adonis* by Pierre-Paul Prud'hon (1800); http://www.wikipaintings.org/en/pierre-paul-prud-hon/venus-und-adonis

Chapter 18. Pyramus and Thisbe: Missed Connections

Highlighted Themes

- Star-crossed lovers
- The consequences of impulsive actions in the name of love

Pivotal Questions

What sorts of barriers are put in the way of "young love" in the modern world? Parental or societal disapproval? Which barriers are useful in our day and age and which are not?

In what ways can people get carried away with their new or young love? What impulsive behaviors crop up and what is the best way to deal with those impulses, in your opinion?

Prominent Literary References

The most famous, of course, is the inadvertently comedic play presented by the rustic "Mechanicals" to the Duke and Hippolyta in act 5 of Shakespeare's *A Midsummer Night's Dream*. The segment is often presented on its own at Renaissance faires and Shakespeare festivals as a bit of fun drama. The same situation is purposely manipulated by the two lovers' parents in the American musical classic *The Fantasticks*.

Similar Motifs in Western Literature

Tales of star-crossed lovers appear repeatedly in Western literature, including but not limited to Shakespeare's *Romeo and Juliet*, Chaucer's "The Merchant's Tale," Willa Cather's novel *O Pioneers!*, and the musical *West Side Story*, among many others.

Paintings

- *Thisbe* by John William Waterhouse (1909);
  http://www.wikipaintings.org/en/john-william-waterhouse/thisbe-1909
- *Pyramus and Thisbe* by Pierre Gautherot (1799);
  http://commons.wikimedia.org/wiki/File:Pierre_Gautherot_-_Pyramus_and_Thisbe,_1799.jpg

Chapter 19. Hero and Leander: Reckless Love

Highlighted Themes

- Destructiveness of blind passion
- The inevitability of fate when lovers take risks

Pivotal Questions

Do modern lovers take the risks that Hero and Leander do in this myth? What sorts of risky behaviors do modern couples engage in for the sake of love, and where do we draw the line?

Prominent Literary References

Elizabethan writer Christopher Marlowe devoted a poem, "Hero and Leander," to the myth. Shakespeare alludes to it in act 4 of *As You Like It*, using the myth to speak of how men only die for love in stories and fictions. Byron's poem, after his own swim through the channel, is called "Written After Swimming from Sestos to Abydos." There are several cantatas and songs based on the myth, one of which is "Ero e Leandro" (1707) by George Frideric Handel.

Paintings

- *Last Watch of Hero* by Frederic Leighton (1880);
  http://en.wikipedia.org/wiki/File:Leightonhero.jpg

Chapter 20. Orpheus and Eurydice: Love and Loss

Highlighted Themes
- Descent into the underworld
- Loss and impatience in love

Pivotal Questions
Orpheus and Eurydice's story begins with a fateful accident. Many relationships are derailed by apparently accidental circumstances. Do either Orpheus or Eurydice have any responsibility for sending their story on its path? Just as their story seems to be getting a happy ending, Orpheus cannot resist the urge to look back and check on Eurydice before they are completely in the clear. Is that because of his anxiety for his love or is it because he can't entirely trust that she is still with him? What do you think? How do couples sometimes make fateful mistakes because of anxiety or worry of each other?

Prominent Literary References
Orpheus Descending, a play by Tennessee Williams (1957), and *Eurydice*, a play by Sarah Ruhl (2003), retell the Orpheus and Eurydice myth. The stage musical *Rent*, the opera *La Bohème*, and the film *Moulin Rouge* all mimic the structure of it. The bohemian world of art, alternative lifestyles, illness, and drug use typically represents the "Underworld" and then usually one central male character represents Orpheus in his descent into that world in order to save his love (usually a beautiful artist). Typically, he loses her but saves her independent and vibrant spirit in his memory and life's work.

Parallel Myths from Other Cultures
The myth of Orpheus and Eurydice parallels the Japanese myth of Izanagi and Izanami, the Mayan myth of Itzamna and Ixchel, and the Indian myth of Savitri and Satyavan.

Paintings
- *Orpheus and Eurydice* by Christian Gottlieb Kratzenstein (1806); http://en.wikipedia.org/wiki/File:Kratzenstein_orpheus.jpg
- *Orpheus Leading Eurydice from the Underworld* by Camille Corot (1861); http://www.wikipaintings.org/en/camille-corot/orpheus-leading-eurydice-from-the-underworld-1861

Chapter 21. Alcestis and Admetus: Lost Love

Highlighted Themes
- Selfishness in marriage
- Knowing what you've lost after you've lost it

- Regretting giving up a marriage for one's own selfish ends
- Sacrifice for a larger purpose—family, honor

Pivotal Questions

Admetus's request to have others give up their lives to save his own is clearly selfish and one sided. Do you think he would have asked such a sacrifice of others if he had known sorrow or loss in his life before? In what ways does Alcestis show forethought in her sacrifice? How is she looking to protect her children rather than simply obey her husband? In what ways does marriage sometimes ask unreasonable sacrifices of each partner? And how are marriage partners changed after such sacrifices have been made? How do they move forward?

Prominent Literary References

Euripides wrote the tragedy *Alcestis*. There are two operas based on Alcestis's story, one by Handel and one by Gluck. Two plays—*Alcestis* by H. P. Lovecraft and *A Life in the Sun* by Thornton Wilder—were based on the myth and on Euripides's play.

Paintings

- *Death of Alcestis* by Angelica Kauffman (date unknown); http://en.wikipedia.org/wiki/File:Alcesti.jpg

Chapter 22. Cephalus and Procris: Toxic Love

Highlighted Themes

- Destructiveness of jealousy
- Duplicity and faithlessness

Pivotal Questions

The term "toxic relationship" is often used to describe couples whose negative feelings and compulsions overtake their best intentions. In what ways is Cephalus's and Procris's jealousy and suspicion still a problem in modern relationships? How do Cephalus and Procris set each other up for failure in their relationship? Do you believe they would ever learn to trust each other and be faithful or would their personal demons constantly sabotage their relationship?

Prominent Literary References

There are many similar motifs to this story in Western literature. In particular, in Shakespeare's *Othello*, Othello is jealous toward his wife, Desdemona, who is chaste, but he believes her to be unfaithful. Desdemona also dies at the hands of her husband.

Paintings
- *Cephalus and Procris* by Paolo Veronese (1580);
  http://www.wikipaintings.org/en/paolo-veronese/cephalus-and-procris

Chapter 23. Acontius and Cydippe: A Marriage of True Minds

Highlighted Themes
- Wit and trickiness in courtship

Pivotal Questions
Some view Acontius's method of winning a bride as clever. Others view it as duplicitous. What do you think? How would a modern romantic movie treat this story? In the modern world, how would a woman respond to being tricked and enduring illness after illness? Would that be a deal breaker, or would she give the relationship a chance because everything worked out "all right in the end"?

Paintings
- *Cydippe with Acontius's Apple* by Paulus Bor (circa 1640);
  http://commons.wikimedia.org/wiki/File:Paulus_Bor_001.jpg

Chapter 24. Ceyx and Alcyone: Calming the Waters

Highlighted Themes
- The transformative power of love and grief
- The bond among a truly loving couple

Pivotal Questions
What traits in their relationship do you think Ceyx and Alcyone have that make them worthy of everlasting love together? Are those traits a myth in the modern world? The couple was granted a transformation after Ceyx's death—how does this parallel modern spiritual ideas about love in the afterlife?

Paintings
- *Halcyone* by Herbert James Draper (1915);
  _http://en.wikipedia.org/wiki/File:Herbert_James_Draper_-_Halcyone_(1915).jpg

Chapter 25. Baucis and Philemon: Love at the End

Highlighted Themes
- Mature and committed love
- Devotion to the end of life

Pivotal Questions

Baucis and Philemon had obviously lived a full, humble life together, "fully attuned to each other." What skills or traits do you imagine they must have had to have lived together for so long, so well? What does their example of hospitality say about them, as opposed to their neighbors? Would you rather die at the same moment as your soul mate, so you wouldn't see each other's graves? Or would you rather that each of you live all of your appointed days, even if at the end you are alone?

Prominent Literary References

Shakespeare references this story in *Much Ado About Nothing* (act 2, scene 1) and in *As You Like It* (act 3, scene 3). Charles Frazier retells the myth in the final chapter of his novel *Cold Mountain* (2006).

Paintings

- *Philemon and his wife Baucis hospitably entertain Jupiter and Mercury in travellers' guise* by Hendrick Goudt (circa 1620–30); http://commons.wikimedia.org/wiki/File:Hendrick_Goudt_-_Jupiter_en_Hermes_bij_Philemon_en_Baucis.jpg

Index

Acontius, 121-126
Acrisios, 51-52
Admetus, 106-112
Adonis, 84, 85-90
  Gardens of, 88
  paintings of, 89
AEetes, 58
Aegeus, 56
Aeneas, 62-69
Aeneid, 63, 69
Aeolus, 74-77,
  127-128, 131
Agamemnon, 31,
  79
Agelaus, 24
Alcestis, 106-112
  Death, 110-111
Alcestis, 108-111
Alcyone, 127-133
Alcmene, 50
Allen, Woody, 42
Amphitryon, 50
Anchises, 63
Androgeus, 56
Anna, 66, 68
Antinous, 46
Antony, Mark, 77
Aphrodite, 11, 22,
  24, 35, 46, 71-72,
  87-88, 97
Apollo, 89-90, 101,
  107-108, 128
Apuleius, Lucius,
  12-14

Ares, 77
Argo, 58
Ariadne, 5, 55-62,
  69
  paintings of,
  60-61
Ariosto, Ludovico,
  62
Aristaeus, 102
Arnobius of Sicca,
  72
Artemis, 6, 10-11,
  31, 35, 107,
  121-122, 125, 128
Asclepius, 107
Athena, 1, 22, 24
Aurora, 113-114,
  116-117, 119
Bacchus, 60-61,
Baer, Karl, 45, 48
Baucis, 134-137
Bellini, 94
Beauty and the
  Beast, 13
Bisexualty in the
  Ancient World, 47
Body, N.O., 45, 48
Boucher, François,
  19
Bulfinch, Thomas,
  93, 115
Bulfinch's
  Mythology, 93, 115
Butades, 70
Byron, 99

Byron Swim, 99
Caesar, Julius, 77
Caligula, 77
Callimachus, 122
Calliope, 102
Calypso, 62, 69
Canace, 74-78
Cantarella, Eva, 47
Castor, 16-18
Catallus, 57
Cenchreis, 80
Cephalus, 113-120
  test of chastity,
  118-120
Cerebus, 103
Ceres, 82
Ceyx, 127-133
Charon, 103
Chione, 128, 133
Chrysippus, 89
Cinderella, 13-14
Cinyras, 79-84
Circe, 62
Clement of
  Alexandria, 72
Cleopatra, 77
Clytemnestra,
  16-18, 79
Corona Borealis, 60
Correggio, 18
Cranach, 25
Cupid, 12-15, 18,
  35, 53, 68, 81
Cyclopes, 107

Cydippe, 121-126
"Cydippe", 122
Da Vinci,
Leonardo, 18
Daedalion,
127-128, 133
Daedalus, 55
Danaë, 50-53
    paintings of,
    52-53
Dante, 3
Deion, 113
Deiphobus, 27
Demeter/Ceres, 77
Desire Under the
Elms, 9-10
Diana, 6, 31, 35, 86,
117, 122-124
Dido, 62-69
Dido, Queen of
Carthage, 67
Dionysus/Zagreus,
101-102, 105
Drusilla, 77
Echo, 39-40
Electra Complex,
79-80
Elliot, T.S., 2
Endymion, 89
Eosophorus/
Lucifer, 127
(The) Epistles of
Ovid, 124
Erechtheus, 113
Eris, 21
Eurydice/Aganippe,
51, 101-105
Euripides,
    Alcestis, 108-111

Helen, 17, 20,
27-28
Hippolytus, 5-7,
9-11
Europa, 51, 54
Faerie Queene, 63
(The) Fantasticks,
93
Fates, 108-110
Female sexuality,
3-4
First Vatican
Mythographer, 17
Freud, Sigmund, 1,
8, 79-80
Furies, 81
Galatea, 73
Ganymede, 46, 89,
89
Gemini, 16
Gentilesci,
Artemisia, 53
Georgics, 102, 104
Gerusalemme
Liberata, 62
Golden Fleece, 16,
58-59
Gounod, 94
Hades, 88, 103, 107
Hadrian, 46
"Halcyon", 130-131
Hector, 25, 32-33
Hecuba, 24
Helen, 17, 20,
27-28, 125
Helen (of Troy), 16,
21-28, 55
    birth, 17-18
    kidnapping,
    25-27

Hepburn,
Katharine, 126
Hera, 2-4, 22, 24,
27, 54, 77, 123, 127
Heracles, 89, 111
Hermaphrodites,
37-38, 45
Hermaphroditus, 2,
35-39, 89
Hermes, 22, 24, 35,
62, 128
Hermione, 23, 111
Hero, 96-100, 128,
132-133
"Hero and
Leander", 99
Heroides, 7-8,
30-34, 74, 76, 96,
99-100, 122, 125
Hesiod, 127, 131
Hippolytus, 5-11
Hippolytus, 5-7,
9-11
Homer, 31
    Iliad, 16, 25-26,
    29-30
    Odyssey, 16
Homosexuality, 40,
46, 48, 89-90
    female, 46-47
Hyancinthus, 89
Hyginus, 89
Hylas, 89
I Capuleti e i
Montecchi, 94
Ianthe, 43-49
Iarbus, 64, 66
Icarus, 55
incest, 76-78, 80-84
Iliad, 16, 25-26,
29-30

Inferno, 3
Iphigenia, 31
Iphis, 43-49
Isis, 44, 47
Jason, 16, 58-60
Jung, Carl, 79
Juno, 68, 77, 127, 130
Jupiter, 50, 68, 77, 89, 127, 134, 136
Kane, Sarah, 8-10
Klimt, Gustav, 53
Labyrinth, 55-57, 59
Laodamia, 29-34
Leander, 96-100, 128, 132-133
Leda, 16-20, 22, 50-51, 55
   paintings of, 18-20
"Leda and the Swan," 20
Leontes, 111
Liberalis, Antoninus, 117
Ligdus, 44-44
Lucian, 130
Macareus, 74-78
Manto, 3
Marlowe, Christopher, 25, 67, 99
Mars, 77, 90
Masturbation, 42
Medea, 58-60, 62
Medea, 59-60
Medusa, 52
Memoirs of a Man's Maiden Years, 45

Menelaus, 23, 25, 27
Mercouri, Melina, 59-60
Mercury, 35, 69, 134, 136
Metamorphoses, 30, 35-36, 43, 85, 88, 104-105, 114, 134-135
   3, 41
   4, 36
   8, 137
   9, 48
   10, 80-81, 83
   11, 129, 132
Michelangelo, 18
(A) Midsummer's Night Dream, 93
Minos, 5, 54-58, 116-117
Minotaur, 5, 55-57
Morpheus, 130
Musaeus, 97
Myrrha, 79-84
Narcissus, 39-42, 89
Natural History, 70
Nemesis, 17
Never on Sunday, 59-60
Night, 18
Ninus, 91
Noah, 134
O'Neill, Eugene, 9-10
Odysseus, 62-64, 69, 130
Odyssey, 16, 62, 69
Oeagrus of Thrace, 101

Oedipus, 1
Oedipus, 1, 8, 44, 79
   complex, 24, 41
Oenone, 24
Oracle of Delphi, 51, 124-125
Orestes, 79
Orlando, 2-3
Orlando Furioso, 62
Orpheus, 81, 101-105, 110
Ovid, 71, 73, 89-90, 132
   (The) Epistles of Ovid, 124
   Heroides, 7-8, 30-34, 74, 76, 96, 99-100, 122-123, 125
   Metamorphoses, 30, 35-36, 41, 43, 48, 80-81, 83, 85, 88, 104-105, 114, 129, 132, 134-135, 137
Paris, 21-28, 44, 125
   paintings of, 25
   prophesy regarding, 24, 26
Parrhasius, 71
Pasiphaë, 5, 46, 54-56, 116-117
Peleus, 21
Pelias, 107
Penelope, 130
Persephone/ Proserpina, 77, 87-88, 103
Perseus, 52
Phaedra, 5-11
   suicide/death, 9-10

Phaedra, 7, 9
Phaedra's Love, 8-10
Phédre, 7-9
Philemon, 134-137
Philonoe, 16
Philostephanus, 71-72
Phoebe, 16
Plato, 130
Pliny the Elder, 70
Pollux, 16-18
Poseidon, 6, 54, 74
Poussin, 89, 89
Priam, 24
Procris, 113-120
    chastity, test of, 115-117
Propoetides, 71
Protesilaus, 29-34
Pseudo-Apollodorus, 17, 87, 127, 131
Psyche, 12-13, 83
Pygmalion (brother of Dido), 64, 66
Pygmalion (sculptor), 34, 70-73
Pygmalion, 72
Pyramus, 91-95
Racine, Jean, 7
Romeo and Juliet, 75, 93-94
Roméo et Juliette, 94
Rubens, 89
Salmacis, 35-40
Sappho, 46
Seneca the Younger, 5, 7, 9

Shakespeare, William, 75, 86, 89-90, 93-94, 111, 121, 126
Shaw, George Bernard, 72
Sichaeus/Acerbas, 64, 69
Simon, Hermann, 45
Sisyphus, 103
Sleeping Beauty, 24
Spenser, Edmund, 63
Strophe, 8
Suetonius, 77
Tasso, Torquato, 62
Telethusa, 43-44, 47
Theoclymenus, 28
Theseus, 5-7, 22-23, 56-61, 69
    slaying of the Minotaur, 57-59
Thetis, 21
Thisbe, 91-95
Tiersias, 1-4
Timandra, 16
Tintoretto, 19
Titans, 102
Titian, 89
    painting of Ariadne, 60-61
    painting of Danaë, 53
Tracy, Spencer, 126
(The) Tragical History of the Life and Death of Doctor Faustus, 25

(The) Transformations of Lucius/The Golden Ass, 12
Trojan Horse, 26
Trojan War, 22-28, 29-34, 65, 121
Tyndareus, 16-17, 22-23
Venus, 8, 14-15, 35, 53, 63, 68, 71, 84-90, 97-98
"Venus and Adonis," 89-90
Venus and Adonis, 86
Veronese, 89
Virgil,
    Aeneid, 63, 69
    Georgics, 102, 104
(The) Waste Land, 2
West Side Story, 94
Winter's Tale, 111
Woolf, Virginia, 2-3
Xenophanes, 50, 52
Yeats, William Butler, 20
Zeus, 1-4, 22, 46, 52, 68-69, 77, 88, 107, 123, 127
    as a swan, 16-20, 50-51, 54
    as a bull, 51, 54
Zeuxis, 71, 73

Acknowledgements

From Ruth K. Westheimer
To the memory of my entire family who perished during the Holocaust. To the memory of my late husband, Fred, who encouraged me in all my endeavors. To my current family, my daughter Miriam Westheimer, EdD, son-in-law Joel Einleger, MBA, their children Ari and Leora, my son Joel Westheimer, PhD, daughter-in-law Barbara Leckie, PhD, and their children Michal and Benjamin. I have the best grandchildren in the entire world!

Jerry Singerman, PhD—without his knowledge, skill, and friendship this book would not have been born. Thank you, thank you. And thanks to Jerry's wife, Liliane Weissberg, for "lending" Jerry to me for this project. A special thanks also goes to Pierre Lehu, my Minister of Communications for the past thirty years, and to my publisher and friend, Kent Sorsky.

Thanks to all the many family members and friends for adding so much to my life. I'd need an entire chapter to list them all, but some must be mentioned here: David Best, MD, Chuck Blazer, Amos Grunebaum, MD, David Hryck, Esq., Rabbi and Mrs. Barry Katz, Bonnie Kaye, Marga and Bill Kunreuther, Steve Lassonde, PhD, Matthew and Vivian Lazar, Rabbi and Mrs. William Lebeau, Rabbi and Mrs. James Ponet, Cliff Rubin, Daniel Schwartz, Joanne Seminara, Esq., Dr. and Mrs. William Sledge, and Jeffrey and Marilyn Tabak, Esq.

Finally, I'd like to thank the following friends and colleagues for all they've done for me: Peter Banks, MD, Jeff Belle, Jaguar Bennett, Gwynne Bloomfield-Pike, Frank Chervenak, MD, Richard Cohen, MD, Cynthia and Howard Epstein, Mayer Glaser, PhD, Polly and Herman Hochberg, Steve Kaplan, PhD, Patti Kenner, Robert Krasner, MD, Robin and Rosemary Leckie, Hope J. Leichter, PhD, John and Giner Lollos, Jeff and Nancy Jane Loewy, Sanford Lopater, Jed Lyons, David Marwell, Steve Mettee, Peter Niculescu, Niko Pfund, Leslie Rahl, Bob and Yvette Rose, Cliff and Eleanor Rubin, Debra Jo Rupp, Mark St. Germain, Amir Shaviv, David Simon, MD, and Shkurte Tonaj.

From Jerome E. Singerman
My thanks to Ruth K. Westheimer, the most exuberant, persistent, and probing collaborator and the best of friends. Without her this book would not exist. To my mother, whose good humor and optimism I did not inherit, and to my late father, whose temperament I probably did. To my brother, who preceded me into the family, and to Irving Kittay, who followed decades later, and to the memory of Roman and Ula Weissberg, who would, I hope, have enjoyed all this. And to Liliane, of course, who proves every day that love is no myth.

About the Authors

Dr. Ruth K. Westheimer is one of America's best-known names in relationship therapy. Widely known for her honest and humane approach to human sexuality, Westheimer pioneered frank sex advice on radio with her program *Sexually Speaking*, which premiered in 1980 on WYNY in New York. Since then Westheimer has become America's favorite sex expert, giving help to millions through radio, television, newspapers, magazines, books and her website, **DrRuth.com**.

Dr. Westheimer has taught at New York Hospital-Cornell University Medical Center, Lehman College, Brooklyn College, Adelphi University, Columbia University and West Point. She is currently an adjunct professor at New York University and a fellow of Calhoun College at Yale, Butler College at Princeton and the New York Academy of Medicine. Dr. Westheimer has her own private practice in New York and lectures worldwide. She is the author of over 35 books, including *Dr. Ruth's Sex After 50* (Quill Driver Books, 2005) and *Dr. Ruth's Guide for the Alzheimer's Caregiver* (Quill Driver Books, 2012).

Jerome E. Singerman is a book editor who lives in Philadelphia, Pennsylvania. He holds a doctorate in comparative literature from Harvard University and he has taught literature at Harvard, Bates College, and the Maryland Institute College of Art. Singerman is the author of *Under Clouds of Poesy: Poetry and Truth in French and English Reworkings of the Aeneid, 1160–1513*.